# Choosing the Right School for Your Child

**BRANDI ROTH, Ph.D**

**FAY VAN DER KAR-LEVINSON, Ph.D**

**Association of Ideas Publishing**

**Beverly Hills, California**

**Association of Ideas Publishing**

Brandi Roth, Ph.D.

433 North Camden Drive, Suite 1128

Beverly Hills, CA 90210

Cover design by Kathleen Lowry

Roth, Ph.D., Brandi

   Choosing the Right School for Your Child/by Brandi Roth, Ph.D. and Fay Van Der Kar-Levinson, Ph.D.

   ISBN 0-9647119-0-7

1. School Choices in Education

2. Elementary and Secondary Education

3. Parent Participation Handbook

Library of Congress Catalog Card Number: 95-78499

Manufactured in the United States of America

06  05  04  03  02  01  00  99  98        10  9  8  7  6  5  4  3  2

# ACKNOWLEDGEMENTS

We gratefully acknowledge the support and inspiration provided by our families, friends, and colleagues.

Your insights and your stories of school successes and failures all enriched this book.

We dedicate this book to the many families who so diligently strive to choose the right school for their child.

# TABLE OF CONTENTS

Understanding Your Child
Learning Styles
Evaluating Your Child
Readiness for School/Kindergarten
Retention
Family Style and School Style

Academic Curricula
School's Educational Philosophy
Teachers and Other Staff
Class Size
Classmates
Special Characteristics of the School
Parental Involvement
Physical Facilities

# INTRODUCTION

Selecting the best school for your child can be an exciting search involving adventure and self-discovery for both you and your child. Yes, the challenge of school interviews and application forms might be daunting and confusing, but our simple suggestions can guide you through the process. Let us help by explaining the mysteries of selecting a school and by offering guidance and support every step of the way. We've assisted hundreds of parents in our practices and can offer you the assistance that will turn any anxiety you may feel into an adventure — perhaps even fun.

Our book is one of the first written to encourage parents to become knowledgeable about their children's schools in a systematic, and organized way. It can help you make the best possible school choices for your child. We will provide information about the many different kinds of schools available today: private schools, neighborhood public schools, and some of the many special programs offered by the public school systems, such as magnet schools.

This book is also valuable for parents who are not involved in choosing a school right now but want to become more informed about the ongoing education of their children, about its specific programs and processes.

Our clients have described us as similar to restaurant critics, keeping on top of the field by continuing to research the ever changing menu choices.

As psychologists, we are trained to deal with anxieties, including the anxiety often caused by the process of choosing a school. Information is the best way to deal with anxiety. We provide information that can empower you on two levels: learning to evaluate schools and their styles of learning, and learning to evaluate which kind of setting will be best for your child.

Years of experience in evaluating and helping to select superior schools has taught us just what to look for. We pass this information on to you by providing a checklist of questions to ask when you visit a school. These questions will help you evaluate everything from the play area to the teaching staff, helping you avoid costly mistakes by alerting you to everything you must know before enrolling.

For the parents who are investigating the private school option, this book is an invaluable guide through the bewildering variety of choices. For parents concerned with finding quality education in the public school system at a time when many public school programs for gifted students are being cut back or eliminated, this book will help you discover exactly what programs are available to your child.

We believe that parents must be involved in their children's education; to do so most effectively, parents must learn as much as possible about the current state of education. This means understanding who your children are and understanding their educational needs.

## CHAPTER 1

# PUBLIC OR PRIVATE: CHOOSING FOR YOUR CHILD

As a parent, you are eager to help your child find the "right" school, the one that will provide a successful educational experience.  In this chapter, we will focus on the basic issue of public school as opposed to private school.

Perhaps your choices begin with the *nearest public school*.  In addition, your public school system probably offers specialized or so-called *"magnet" schools* that draw students from all over your town or city and stress a particular area of education or cater to students with particular needs. Next, you probably live within commuting distance of one or more *private schools*.  They may have built reputations based upon the social status of their students, their belief in single-sex education or their concentration on college preparatory subjects.  The private school known as a *"parochial" school* is associated with a religious belief or institution.

Your choice between a public school, a magnet school, a parochial school, or a private school will have lifetime consequences for your child. It will be one of your major decisions as a parent.

**POSITIVE ATTITUDE HINT:**  Please understand that we do not see one type of school as "better" than any other in itself.  We were both educated in the public schools, yet many of our clients do best in the private school environment.  Your choice will depend first and foremost on the individual needs and aspirations of your child.

Your decision has a long history. Americans first faced the issue of private "versus" public schools more than 100 years before the Revolution. The earliest public schools in the U. S. were established in 1647 when the Puritan colony of Massachusetts required all towns with 50 families to hire a schoolteacher to educate their children. The intent of these public, tax-supported schools, was to ensure that children from all social and economic backgrounds studied the Bible. At the same time, churches and individual families in colonies outside New England began establishing private schools. Since these schools charged a fee for each pupil, only the children of wealthier families could afford to enroll. Nearly three and a half centuries later, American parents are still having to cope with the difficult questions raised by the two-track system set up by our 17th century forefathers.

Currently there are 47 million students enrolled in elementary, middle and secondary schools in the United States. The vast majority, almost 42 million, attend public schools; 5 million are in non-public schools, both independent and parochial. According to the National Association of Independent Schools, there were almost 400,000 students enrolled in independent schools in the 1991-92 academic year.

The private school population has continued to increase in recent years despite the downturn in the economy and a smaller demographic base. More families from different economic, social, and religious backgrounds are enrolling their children in independent schools than ever before — an increase that is expected to continue at least through the turn of the century. Yet at the same time, many parents feel a strong commitment to public school education. They cite a variety of factors influencing their decision, particularly the high cost of private school tuition and the air of social elitism sometimes associated with a private school education.

## TODAY'S NEW EDUCATIONAL AWARENESS

Until quite recently, the educational focus was solely on the child's performance in academics. Failure to memorize an assignment or to produce a report on time often resulted in humiliation (the dunce cap), physical punishment (the paddle), suspension or expulsion. The child's motivation to learn was primarily the avoidance of punishment.

The price some children paid for their academic education was a lifetime of psychological harm and the failure to build during their school years the social skills that we all need throughout life. In addition, many children were denied the opportunity at school to develop physical skills, teamwork abilities, and sportsmanship from physical education classes.

Today we are at an educational crossroads. Parents and teachers are becoming increasingly aware that a *positive educational experience is more than academic learning*. But what is the best way to balance the many different potentials for development — social skills, athletic achievement, academic learning — in order to serve your child's best interests?

Properly matching your child with a school will help ensure that he/she receives a *sound academic education*...

will have enhanced opportunities for *psychological well-being* and growth...

will learn *socialization skills* from her classmates, other friends and the parents of classmates...

will develop skills and interests in *physical activities* that will result in a lifetime of improved physical well being...

and will reach her potential for the *highest moral development* and behavior.

To put it more succinctly, the best possible educational experience will focus on the following five fundamental goals, which will be helpful to keep in mind as you evaluate the different schools available to you:

**FIVE FUNDAMENTAL GOALS:**

1.  A solid academic education

2.  A psychologically positive educational experience

3.  A socially positive educational experience

4.    A physically positive educational experience

5.    A morally positive educational experience

## YOU *CAN* DO IT:

You will select the best school by *learning as much as possible about the school* and by *understanding the unique characteristics of your child*.   The evaluation and selection of schools is discussed in greater detail in Chapters 4 and 5.   Coming to a better understanding of your child's special characteristics is discussed in Chapter 3.

Concern, investigation and common sense will produce immediate, substantial and ongoing benefits. Our suggested step-by-step approach will allow you to do everything possible to help your child build for his future:

1.    First, *evaluate* the schools and your child.

2.    Then make the *best match* between the school's characteristics and your child's needs.

3.    Finally, *prepare yourself* to participate fully in the ongoing educational experience.

Quite often, our clients arrive at our offices in a perplexed state of mind.   For many parents, the challenge of making the right educational decisions for their child can become confusing and frightening.   We hope that the gift and message of this book will be the *specific guidelines* we provide throughout in order to take the guesswork out of decision making as you plan for your child's future.   These guidelines have developed out of our many experiences with parents who are dealing with the realities of selecting among schools.

**POSITIVE ATTITUDE HINT:**  The key word in making a match of  school and child is "best", but the meaning of "best" can change dramatically.   For example, what is best for your child at the elementary level might not be useful at the secondary or college level.   You will need to constantly re-evaluate your child's program from kindergarten on.

Your decision whether to send your child to public or to private school may reveal as much about you and your family's self-image and values as the neighborhood you've chosen to live in or the careers and other interests you pursue. Not surprisingly, the decision has been a watershed in many marriages, especially **when spouses take opposing sides**. We have seen the ensuing disagreements reveal prejudices that neither partner had ever acknowledged to the other before.

For **parents whose own identities are often defined by their children's accomplishments**, the issue is even more complicated. Some may believe that a public school education is a social stigma that will undermine their child's chance of professional success later in life. Some parents may believe that a school choice reflects their social status. As a consequence, they may become determined to enroll their children in the private school of their own choice without considering whether or not it is the best place for the student.

**CASE STUDY**: A 15-year old client, Amy, was automatically enrolled in an exclusive private girls' school where her older sister was a successful, well-adjusted and well-liked student. Moreover, their father was on the board of directors. Amy, too tall for her age, too gangly to wear clothes well, was miserable. Whereas her sister was very verbal and self-confident, Amy was shy, reflective and suited by nature to a less competitive environment. Her school experience was a disaster.

In this case, an emphasis on family tradition superseded Amy's emotional and academic needs. When her parents took our advice and transferred her to a public school in their community, she became much happier. Her experience illustrates that parents cannot make automatic assumptions about the advisability of private education.

## FACTS TO CONSIDER FOR YOUR CHILD'S BEST INTERESTS

To repeat: You are choosing for your child and your child's future, not for your own needs.

Therefore, it is important to approach the "public vs. private" question with **an open mind**. Too often parents are already prejudiced in favor of one educational system over another before they consider all of the options available in the community. These options have probably expanded since you last looked. In addition, changes have undoubtedly taken place in schools that you thought you knew well when you were school-age yourself: new kinds of instruction, improved physical facilities, a more diverse student body.

The following checklist will help you focus your thinking:

1.  *Cost*:  Can we afford the yearly tuition of a private school — and other costs — without seriously compromising the family's financial situation and basic lifestyle?

2.  *Educational opportunities, specialties or additional opportunities*: What do the public and private schools in our community offer their students, including after-school and special programs for both the gifted and the learning delayed/disabled?

3.  *Location*:  Where are the public and private schools in our community located?  What is the cost of the bus service at a private school?  How much time will it take to drive my child to school in another area of our community?

Many other factors will come into play in your final decision, as you will see in later chapters, but let's focus now on the general distinctions between public and private school education.

As we do so, keep in mind that there is a wide range of quality in both public and private schools.  Depending upon your community, you may be near a public school that has more National Merit Scholars than any other school, public or private, in the state.  Or a private school may have an educational philosophy that puts academic achievement second or third on the list of its goals for students.

## PUBLIC SCHOOLS — THE OVERALL PICTURE

If you tend to feel dismissive toward public education, be aware that there are *many ways to make public schools work for the individual needs of your child*.

Today, more public schools than ever before are offering a variety of alternative programs.  Too often, parents tend to overlook such enrichment options as accelerated programs for the gifted or magnet schools devoted to a single area: science, mathematics, performing arts, computers, the visual arts.  There are also alternative schools within the public schools system for children who do not respond well to the conventional academic environment.

If your child has a learning disability, specialized help is available at no additional cost to your family. After-school care in the form of extended school days is available. This service is important for working parents, many of whom find private after-school day care to be prohibitively expensive.

Also on the plus side, there is the convenience of sending your child to a community school that is often within walking distance of your home. When a longer commute is necessary, you can use the public school bus service.

And there is the basic financial consideration: Thanks to the vision of our forefathers, all school-age children can be assured of a public education from kindergarten through senior high school at no additional tuition cost for their families.

Because your child's nearest public school is probably close to or located in your immediate neighborhood, he will form closer bonds during the school day with his neighborhood friends. Aside from sharing the same classes, they will also take part in the same athletic, social, and after-school activities.

This proximity between school and neighborhood also reinforces the bond between neighbors. Making sure their children are getting the best education available brings parents together with a common goal. Because your local public school may reflect a cross-section of your community, you are likely to find other parents who have your same interests and background. For many families the public school community reflects the values and concerns of their households. Parents who feel a strong tie with the community find that the bond is strengthened by their children's enrollment in the neighborhood public school.

**POSITIVE ATTITUDE HINT:** Remember that generations of children who grew up in public schools have gone on to achieve their goals, including higher education, and have led satisfying lives.

There are many very sound reasons for choosing a public school as best for your child's education. There are *also disadvantages* that have been well-documented. It is wise to consider them, too, before making your final decision, since many of them strike at the bedrock of the public school system in this country.

By definition, public schools depend on public financing. Even in the best of economic times, there is rarely enough money available to provide the educational services our children deserve.

Many public schools do not have enough money for books and other supplies. Classrooms are often overcrowded to the bursting point, making individualized attention impossible. Buildings and grounds may be poorly maintained. Teacher's salaries are low, as is their morale. Some of the most talented and dedicated educators leave the public school system, victims of burnout and economic fatigue. The result is a domino effect, leaving our children the ultimate victims. Often those students who need help the most fall through the cracks and end up dropping out in record numbers.

Because of financial pressures in some communities, even the accelerated programs for the gifted students are being trimmed or eliminated as a cost-cutting measure because such advanced courses may affect less than 5% of the student body. This trend is part of a nationwide pattern that will leave many of our best and brightest students unchallenged, bored and frustrated. We are on the verge of producing a nation of underachievers.

In the worst public school situations, as anyone knows who reads a newspaper or tunes in to news broadcasts, violence can rise to levels that are life-threatening. Chaos in the classroom and halls can make learning impossible. Lax security can lead to on-campus problems with drug abuse. The influx of immigrant children who cannot communicate in English can overwhelm the school's ability to serve their interests and those of the other children at the same time.

On the one hand, this does not necessarily mean that such serious obstacles to your child's learning, emotional well-being and socialization are necessarily going to occur at the public schools in your community. On the other, do your evaluations of these schools with your eyes wide open. The unthinkable can become the norm before parents are fully aware of it.

**TO SUM UP...**
**PROS OF PUBLIC SCHOOLS:**

- Convenience

- No cost for tuition

- A neighborhood school with neighborhood friends and activities

- Sports

- After-school activities

- No time wasted in commuting

- Multi-cultural exposure

- Reflects the real world

- Federal funding for special education services even if the needs are mild or moderate (resource specialist teachers, adapted physical education, speech and language services)

- Extended day services (after school care)

**CONS OF PUBLIC SCHOOLS:**

- Decreasing, inadequate funding

- Cutbacks in accelerated and enrichment programs

- Possible low teacher morale and burnout

- Large, overcrowded classes

- Violence

- Lax school security

- Language barriers

## PRIVATE SCHOOLS — THE OVERALL PICTURE

**CASE STUDY:**  At a large family gathering, a young upwardly-mobile couple proudly announced that their four year old daughter Serena had just been accepted by an exclusive private school.  There was an embarrassed silence.  All of the other young children in the family were attending public schools — and thriving.  In fact, Serena would be the first child in the entire extended family to enroll in private school. Her grandmother summed up the reaction of many relatives by snorting, "Aren't our schools good enough for you?"  Miffed, the couple answered, "No!"

Today, many parents enroll their children in private schools for one reason alone:  The *expectation of a higher quality of education*.

The National Association of Independent Schools (NAIS) reports an especially dramatic increase in the past 10 years in the number of students enrolled in the lower grades: 55% increase in preschool; 27% more in kindergarten; and 20% more in first and second grades.  Clearly, more students are starting their private school education earlier, bypassing the public school system entirely.

This trend indicates that many parents believe the superior educational value is *worth the financial investment*.  Is it?  One factor to consider is the *small teacher-pupil ratio*.  The NAIS reports a student-teacher ratio of 9.4 to 1; in boarding schools the ratio is 6.8 to 1; in day schools, it is 10.1 to 1.  Compare this to the public school ratio of 17.2 students per teacher.

In addition, there is the greater likelihood of a *stable faculty*.  The public school systems have been frequently beset with strikes or threats of strikes by disgruntled teachers.  Also, the private school may *insulate students from the national trend of decreasing scores on standardized tests*.  Because of the cutbacks in programs for gifted children in the public sector, private schools offer talented students a real opportunity to develop their unusual skills in a *supportive academic environment*.  Even students who are not unusually gifted will benefit from this system.

What about a child who is not capable of doing well within a standard curriculum?   Sometimes private schools offer you an opportunity to have your child's individual needs met.  Such factors as small class size, intense teacher and administrator involvement, and altered curriculum if needed will help serve his *special needs for attention*.  In addition, close observation by the staff will help ensure that he doesn't fall through the cracks. On the other hand, if what you want is compassion, be aware that not every private school can commit to offer that. Discuss your child's needs frankly with the admissions officer or other staff at the school.

For some parents, it is important that private schools confer a certain status on their children — and, by extension, on themselves as well. At the extreme, we've met with parents who consider private school education to be a *guarantee of life on the inside track* of social, educational, and financial respectability. Networking, as many professionals can attest, is an important ingredient in success. It can begin as early as preschool when contacts with fellow students and their families can establish social relationships that last for life.

*Private universities traditionally admit a disproportionately high percentage of students from private academically oriented schools.* A debate exists as to whether this feeder-school phenomenon reflects a preference of the colleges for students from certain prestigious private schools or whether the academically enhanced private schools attract a disproportionately high percentage of academically gifted students. The most probable explanation is that, while school admissions are decided on an individual basis, the students applying from schools known to have high academic standards and a track record of graduates successful at college are considered somewhat more likely to succeed. Therefore, the selection of a feeder school that has a high admission rate to private colleges should be given only limited consideration, but it is still a factor.

But some of the above advantages can be seen as disadvantages from other points of view.

For example, many parents regard the social networking of the private school world as *elitist* and see it as a serious drawback to their child's overall development. They regard these schools as educational "hothouses," cultivating students' intellects in an insulated social environment that does not provide real-life academic and social survival skills. In other words, the very nurturing support system that focuses attention on each child as an individual can work against her best interests, protecting her so much that she remains *unprepared for the real world* as it is and will be. "What will happen to my child when he does not get the specialized attention he has come to depend on?" Or, "Will my daughter still get along with her friends in our neighborhood? It is more racially and socially diverse than the private school she is enrolled in." We hear these concerns voiced repeatedly by parents.

In some private schools, the **curriculum may be so specialized** that children who transfer from other educational environments often find it difficult to adjust, or find themselves at an educational disadvantage when they move on later. For example, when a school focuses too intensely on encouraging its students' creative writing abilities, the children may discover after they graduate or transfer that they are not properly grounded in such basic, essential language arts skills as spelling, punctuation, and grammar.

In other private schools, the **"womb with a view" attitude** prevails. Over-eager to build up each student's sense of self-esteem, these institutions give positive feedback that is so inflated it produces unrealistic expectations on the part of parents and children alike.

The tuition, commonly as much as $10,000 a year in many cities, can be a **serious drain on a family's financial resources**, especially when there is more than one child to educate. This high cost can translate into a **high resentment factor**, too. In other words, the parents have to work harder to provide their children with an expensive education, so they expect to see a return on their investment. They can begin to resent the child who does not win the academic honors that they expect as the appropriate return on their considerable investment. Parents can fail to realize that not all private school students are whiz kids, nor can a downright average student be retooled by even the best school into a superior performer.

In fact, some students with academic problems may need a private tutor or other specialized help. Their parents are likely to complain, "I spend eight thousand dollars a year in tuition and now I have to pay a tutor fifty dollars an hour to help Scott pass his math course. What is the point?" (Perhaps Scott would be the first to agree that money and parental resources are being wasted — but in most cases, no one thinks to ask him his opinion.)

Then there are the **hidden costs**, the ones the school catalog neglects to mention. These can range from fees for obligatory class trips to expected contributions to the school building fund.

**CASE STUDIES:** One financially strapped family described their decision-making to me: "Our older daughter is going to private school, but her younger sister is going to public school. Since we can't afford to send both to prep school, we thought they would benefit by telling each other about their different experiences."

In this case, the family's decision seemed to work out well; each sister responded happily to her own school. In some cases, however, there can be competition between siblings when one is enrolled in the socially or academically prestigious school and the other remains in the community public school. In one family we saw, one son expected to get a new car since his older brother had been sent to an expensive private school. "Why shouldn't they spend as much money on me?" he asked.

Among other problems that private schools present for some children are the *social insecurities*. No sooner has the parent put away his checkbook than he has to cope with a twelve year old child who is upset because his family is not in the same lofty tax bracket as his best friend's family. We counseled one family whose teenage son refused to take part in a class trip to another city because his clothes were not as expensive as his classmates'. Still another child refused to join a carpool because he was embarrassed by his family car: a four year old subcompact did not measure up to the forty-thousand-dollar models being driven by the other parents.

Of course, this emphasis on economic status is not restricted to the private school community. Even so, it is more likely to occur there, and some parents worry about the part it might play in shaping the attitudes of children who find themselves competing with classmates from a much higher economic strata than the friends they grew up with.

## TO SUM UP...
## PROS OF PRIVATE SCHOOLS:

- More individual attention

- Smaller class size

- More programs for enrichment and supplement

- Greater opportunity to nurture specific talents

- More teacher support

- Extended day and curriculum services

## CONS OF PRIVATE SCHOOLS:

- Hothouse environment

- Drain on family income

- Extra working hours or moonlighting for parents

- Social insecurity

## WILL YOU EVER FIND THE PERFECT SCHOOL?

There is *no such thing as a perfect school* — public or private.

What is the best possible school for your child?

1.  As we've noted before, it is the institution that best develops your child's unique talents and meets his or her educational and emotional needs.

2.  The student body is neither so large that the pupils cannot receive individual help nor so small that they feel smothered.

3.  It represents an egalitarian ideal, a perfect cross-section of all social, economic, and academic strata, enabling its students to understand and appreciate the unique contributions made by all people in our society.

4.  It offers students a rigorous education designed to highlight their talents and prepare them for colleges and graduate schools.

5.  It provides classes for the gifted and for students with special needs.

6.  It encourages parents to become involved in shaping the educational process that will have a positive impact on the lives of their children.

7.  The building and equipment are well maintained; textbooks and other learning aides are innovative and exciting.

8. It is fun to learn there in large part because it has a teaching staff of talented, highly paid professionals who are eager to work with all of the students.

9. It is close to your home.

10. It is free.

11. It combines the positives of both a good public and a good private school.

**GOOD ATTITUDE HINT:** In the real world, no school yet exists — or possibly ever will — that combines all or even almost all of these desirable factors. Each of the choices available to your child as you make your ongoing evaluations of schools is going to offer a mixed bag of pluses and minuses.

Even when you think you actually have found the perfect school for your child's needs, you may discover that it is not the answer to all possible problems.

**CASE STUDY:** For example, Valerie's parents transferred her from private school because she seemed stifled by the rigorous, conventional teaching and homogeneous student body. But when she started having trouble in public school, they prejudged the situation, jumping to the conclusion that the school was at fault. During a parent conference, it came to light that their daughter, a very bright child, was racing through her class work so that she could read a book (her favorite past time). The result: she was performing at a lower level than she was capable of. With some discussion and cooperation between child, parents, and teacher, Valerie improved the quality of her work and her grades shot up.

In all likelihood, *a good school, either public or private, does exist in your community*, a school fully capable of providing your child with a solid education that is academically rigorous. And, if you believe, as we do, that a good school teaches the mind, body and soul, it will also be committed to preparing its students to be socially involved, caring citizens.

As concerned parents, you should evaluate all the educational institutions in your community with this definition in mind.

Do not prejudge any school until you have learned as much as you can about its curriculum and philosophy.

In the next chapter, we look at some of the different types of schools, public and private, that you are likely to encounter as your make your search for the best possible school for your child.

## CHAPTER 2

# DIFFERENT KINDS OF SCHOOLS

There are many paths to be taken to a good education, each offering something different from the others. Since it is so critical that you match your child with the right kind of school, how can you confidently identify the aims of any individual school?

In this chapter, we discuss **nine basic types of school** and some **additional programs** that are often available in your public school system. A school might not define itself using our terms exactly, but our thumbnail descriptions can easily be applied to any school you are considering.

For example, most private schools will refer to themselves as college preparatory. Using our definitions, however, you will be able to see that some are more accelerated than others — and therefore more demanding of your child's time and energy. It is not unusual for nightly homework assigned by self-described college prep schools of much the same reputation to vary from one hour a night to four hours or more. Similarly, the college prep private school — or the public school, for that matter — may be managed as either a loosely structured or a highly structured school.

In addition, there can be a bewildering array of different types of school programs. Often, the acronyms used to describe specific programs are no help.

But even though school choices vary so widely, certain characteristics tend to cluster together when we have looked at schools and evaluated them.

The following list of nine different types of schools is our way of describing those characteristics to you:

1.  Highly accelerated

2.  Move-at-your-own-pace

3.  Traditional

4.  Special talent

5.  Middle-of-the-road

6.  Religious

7.  Highly structured, highly disciplined

8.  Loosely structured

9.  College Prep

*No single one of these nine different approaches to education is better than any other.* It is simply a matter of different emphases. Your job is to match your child's talents and needs with the school's approach to learning.

Remember, too, that there will be some overlap between the different kinds of schools that may at first obscure the essential differences. For example, a move-at-your-own-pace school and a loosely structured school may be similar in several respects.

On the other hand, the differences can be crucial. The move-at-your-own-pace school will have a curriculum in place through which your child will move "at her own pace". For example, a Montessori school can be a move-at-your-own-pace school with a sequentially well-defined, structured curriculum that is pre-set. By contrast, the loosely structured school will be child-driven; in other words, the structure comes from the child's environment and personal life rather than from an externally imposed curriculum.

As you look at schools to determine exactly how they fall into these categories, beware of relying upon scare stories or exaggerated reputations founded upon incorrect information or rumor. One of our clients was sure she should avoid a school because "everyone said" that the students were using drugs there. In fact, this deservedly prestigious school was as drug-free as any school can be in our world today.

In Chapters 4 and 5, we will explain in detail how you should use your own information-gathering skills to find out as much as possible about potential schools for your child: for example, interviews with teachers and administrators, requests for written materials, and on-site visits to the school campus. For now, let's learn about the basic categories you are likely to encounter on your search.

## 1. THE HIGHLY ACCELERATED SCHOOL

In this type of school, a rigorous academic program will probably require substantial memorization for success. If your child lacks this skill, you should not be seriously considering applying to this school.

The highly accelerated program is best for the child who has the following qualifications:

1. Academically quick to learn

2. Needs to move at a fast pace in order to avoid boredom

3. Needs to be academically challenged

4. Enjoys competition

5. Is stimulated by bright peers

6. Thrives in an environment that rewards academic success

7. Physically mature

8. Socially mature

9. Emotionally mature

10. Hardworking and industrious

## 2. THE MOVE-AT-YOUR-OWN-PACE SCHOOL

This type of school is preferable for the child who learns best by creating her own projects and working independently but is less fulfilled by working on highly specific teacher-directed activities. These schools, by definition, tend to be loosely structured, but their principal aim is to foster a low-key educational approach under which individual differences among students are allowed and accepted.

Move-at-your-own-pace instruction is most appropriate for the child who can be characterized as follows:

1. Creative and imaginative

2. Self-starting

3. Less socially developed than peers

4. Learns at different rates in different areas

5. Learns by experience rather than memorization

6. Needs individual teaching

7. Needs to be physically involved with learning activities rather than learns primarily from reading and listening.

You might ask yourself the following questions in assessing your child for this type of school:

If my child goes to a progress-at-your-own-rate school for his primary education, how will it affect his options for middle school later?

Without a structured grade-level curriculum, will my child be able to pass standardized tests?

How will I fill in any gaps in my child's learning? (One approach is to go to an educational evaluator or psychologist for an academic evaluation.)

## 3. THE TRADITIONAL SCHOOL

The traditional school focuses on teaching fundamental and basic skills such as spelling, grammar, and mathematics. Students are expected to learn these skills in a sequential way. The school's requirements for success are usually expressed clearly in terms of curriculum goals, examination requirements, and expectations of performance in class.

Familiar as the classic approach to education in America for decades, traditional education has enjoyed a revival recently as part of the movement back to fundamentals.

Your child should do well in this type of school if he can be described as follows:

1.  Responds well to a structured program

2.  Looks to adults to initiate activities

3.  Is not self-directing in interests and activities

4.  Needs external feedback and teacher approval along with grades

5.  Does not require the smallest class size

6.  Enjoys structured athletic activities and team sports

7.  Does best with structured extra-curricular activities and field trips

## 4. THE SPECIAL TALENT SCHOOL

Usually offered at the middle and secondary level, these schools emphasize special talent areas, such as music, arts, science, religion, and foreign language in addition to basic academic subjects.

Your child would benefit from this type of school if she has exhibited the following:

1.  A special talent or interest in one or more of these non-academic areas

2.  A good grasp of education essentials

## 5.  THE MIDDLE-OF-THE-ROAD SCHOOL

It is possible to find a highly structured program that is *not also highly accelerated*.  Moving at a slower pace — not too fast, not too slow — it is a kind of bell curve school.

Such schools are probably not best for children at the extremes — gifted and highly creative, or special needs children.  They are designed for the child who thrives in a well-defined learning situation in which he is expected to perform in a specific concrete manner.  He will get feedback in the form of assignments, and the class work will move at a steady pace.  Religious schools often fall into this category.

A decade ago this was a more typical style of school, whether public and private, but too many schools changed to an accelerated program in order to compete for applicants.  To us, this trend is unfortunate because the middle-of-the-road school met the needs of many children very well.  In particular, it allowed a self-discovery process during adolescence. In highly accelerated schools, by contrast, many students don't have the time to discover who they are as a person.

In addition, many students learn best when time is taken for repetition of concepts.  The middle-of-the-road school is more structured than the move-at-your-own-pace school but not quite as rigorous academically as the highly accelerated schools.  You get a little bit of both.

## 6.  THE RELIGIOUS SCHOOL

A combination of an academic and a religious curriculum is appropriate for children whose families and beliefs are enhanced by this type of education.

There is a great range in the amount of emphasis and time devoted to academics and the amount of emphasis and time devoted to religious training.  There is no general rule which is applicable to all religious schools in terms of academic quality, although they tend to be middle-paced schools with a focus on meeting a wide range of abilities in order to meet the religious needs of their particular group.

One special factor in religious education is the *Dual Curriculum*.  For example, in the case of Jewish education, some classes would be secular and taught in English; religious classes would be given in Hebrew.

In deciding whether or not your child will be comfortable with the special demands of the dual curriculum, consider the following:

1.  The school day is generally longer than average.

2.  If your child's language development is less than the norm for her age, she might have difficulty when classes are given in two languages.

3.  Can your child handle the larger work load that generally comes with dual curriculum?

4.  Keep in mind that religious study may be a serious part of the school's agenda. If your child does not practice that faith, will he feel uncomfortable or pressured? When one of our Roman Catholic clients enrolled her son in a parochial school, he began to consider the priesthood. This was more than she was prepared for.

5.  Sometimes, when the parents are of different religions, their child may enroll in a school affiliated with the faith of one parent. Some people like this situation because it doesn't threaten their religious beliefs but does broaden the child's understanding of the world.

    If you are Jewish, for example, and your child attends an Episcopalian school, you might want to explore the options available to him regarding participation in the chapel services or religious classes.

    You might want to attend some of the programs yourself so that you can help explain the differences in points of view to your child.

## 7. THE HIGHLY STRUCTURED, HIGHLY DISCIPLINED SCHOOL

These types of schools tend to be teacher-directed rather than student-directed. Requirements are usually quite specific: for example, students are expected to complete explicit daily and weekly assignments in a standard manner, without deviation.

Such highly structured schools also tend to be highly disciplined. Students usually have assigned seats in classrooms that are organized according to ability grouping. Classes and other activities are rigidly scheduled. Boundaries of acceptable behavior are usually clearly defined in a public set of rules that are enforced.

If your child functions well in structured situations and doesn't like "down" time or free time, these schools can provide a much more satisfying setting. For many children, as a matter of fact, it's a relief to have a clear schedule set out in front of them.

## 8.  THE LOOSELY STRUCTURED SCHOOL

Loosely structured schools tend to be more child-oriented in terms of developing curricula based on each child's individual needs. Course requirements can be satisfied from a choice of assignments.

Each child moves at her own pace, and the teachers tend to be more sensitive to individual moods and situations. In addition, the daily curriculum may fluctuate according to external events rather than remain tied to a purely academic agenda. For example, after the California earthquake in January of 1994, one loosely structured school spent several weeks focusing on many of the events around the earthquake, studying seismic waves and geologic formations, and choosing classroom activities to help the students absorb this life event.

Loosely structured schools are for a child who is adaptable and thrives on change, enjoys the adventure in learning, and is a self-starter. The child who is not motivated by external rewards will do well in this type of school, as will the child who wants to get involved in process rather than outcome.

These programs also do well for children with highly specialized interests. When a child wants to pursue a project, she can devote her energies fully to that endeavor and expand her learning by bringing together several related academic activities.

A child who is easily distracted will find this type of school a chaotic, confusing environment.

If this type of school sounds appropriate for your child, you might want to consider some important questions that could arise later in his education:

> How will going to this school at the elementary school level affect my child's options for middle school?

How successfully will he be able to transfer to a more structured environment?

Without a structured grade-level curriculum, will he be able to pass standardized tests?

How will I fill in any gaps in basic learning?

## 9. THE COLLEGE PREP SCHOOLS

College prep schools tend to be highly structured and academically more rigorous than other schools. While most middle and upper level schools claim that they are designed to prepare students for college, your *choices may actually be rather narrow* if your child wants to enroll in a high-powered college prep curriculum. At the elementary school level, such programs are extremely rare.

Parents can distinguish between the levels of preparation actually offered by competing schools by obtaining *copies of the curriculum guide or study guide* of each school.

Consider the following questions as you look over these materials:

What college-prep courses are offered, and how rigorous are course requirements?

How many advanced or honors classes are offered, and in how many different subject areas?

How many staff members are involved in the college guidance program?

In regard to the last question, a school that provides one part-time college advisement counselor is not serious about offering college preparation. The average college prep school will have at least *one or two full-time college advisors* on staff. Many schools require that students meet with advisors regularly in order to plan curriculum, outside activities and application strategies directed toward acceptance in the appropriate college.

In addition, a college prep school will be prepared to discuss *financial planning* with students and parents in one-on-one sessions or in general informational meetings. In other words, the most effective college prep school does not only offer accelerated course work; it also engages with you and your child in the decisions you will make about college applications.

## ALTERNATIVE PROGRAMS WITHIN THE PUBLIC SCHOOL SYSTEMS

In addition to these nine types of private schools, other opportunities available to you and your child include several different types of special programs that are frequently offered within public school districts.

Because programs vary within states and within school districts, you can find out which programs are available in your community by contacting local officials. If one of the following programs sounds particularly appropriate for your child, ask specifically if it is available under that name. If not, use our thumbnail description to see if the district offers a program that has similar structure or aims.

### MAGNET SCHOOLS

Magnet schools generally target a specific talent or subject area and bring together students from all over a city or county jurisdiction. In Los Angeles County, for example, there are magnet schools concentrating in business, science, gifted students, highly gifted students and zoo studies.

Most magnet schools accept applications and determine admission using eligibility criteria and a lottery system. Ethnic balance in the community may also be a factor.

### GATE PROGRAM

GATE, or Gifted and Talented Education, is a nationwide, federally funded program generally available only for elementary aged children at designated public schools. To qualify, a child has to be identified as gifted by a school administrator then evaluated in a battery of tests generally administered by a school psychologist.

Although criteria for admission may vary from place to place, it is usually based on three things: the results of the tests, recommendation by a teacher, and past academic performance. Sometimes a child can be accepted into GATE when only two out of the three of these criteria are strong.

## HONORS PROGRAMS

Honors programs have been created especially for those children who tend to get good grades, have positive attitudes about school, and thus come highly recommended by their teachers. Honors programs are usually offered at the high school level in both public and private schools, but some middle schools do provide such programs. At the middle school level, the Honors Program may be made available in addition to a Gifted Program. Sometimes, they overlap.

In certain communities, the mix of gifted students and committed instructors, combined with the support of the district, can produce an Honors Program equal or superior to any academic programs available in the most prestigious private schools. For the well-motivated student, this option is worth investigating in depth.

## SPECIAL EDUCATION PROGRAMS

Children with special needs are served by these programs. Usually, it is the school psychologist who identifies and evaluates which students would benefit from this service.

The Special Education Programs most commonly available in public school systems include the following:

1.  Resource Specialist Program (RSP)
    RSP is for a child with normal intelligence who needs supplemental services in math, reading, spelling, and other basics. This program probably takes one hour a day, up to five hours a week. To qualify, children generally need to be two years below grade level or below their peers in performance or ability in a specific academic area.

2.  Speech and Language Services

3.  Adaptive Physical Education

4.  Counseling

5.  Support Services for the physically handicapped who are mainstreamed into the regular classroom.

Because these programs will *not be offered by every school* in your area, you will need to contact school officials to find out where the nearest services are available.  Research is crucial in this arena.

## SPECIAL SCHOOLS

In addition to the special needs programs within public schools, some communities provide special schools for children with exceptional needs.  Such institutions offer special day classes for emotionally disturbed children, mentally retarded children, deaf and hard-of-hearing children, aphasic children, and others who benefit from increased attention from teachers professionally trained in these areas of need.

## CHARTER SCHOOLS

According to a Los Angeles City Schools statement,

> "A charter school is a school which is organized by a group of teachers, community members, parents or others and sponsored by an existing local school board or a county board of education.  The specific goals and operating procedures would be spelled out in the agreement between the board and the organizers, but the school is freed from most state statutes and regulations."

In other words, the "charter school" offers independence to an organization with well-defined educational aims.  In effect, a school district says: Try it, we'll guide you.  The group takes charge of curriculum, but the school system pays salaries and oversees other fiscal details.  As the years go by and the school proves itself, it achieves more and more autonomy.  This is a very promising option that has already gained acceptance in many communities.

In one Southern California community, for example, where the community applied for and gained charter status for their high school, the middle school has become a magnet program and two of the local elementary schools have been granted charter status.  One immediate result is that many parents have pulled their children out of private schools and transferred them back into this exciting, promising new arena.  At the same time, community morale has been boosted, the neighborhoods have stabilized, and perhaps property values might even increase because of the improved school system.  But it took determined, demanding parents to put this together. It was not something mandated by administrators.

In similar vein, there are many parent-led movements within the public schools systems aimed at improving the schools. We may be in a time of dramatic educational reforms and historic changes in public education. For example, the Beverly Hills School District is moving forward with what it calls the Strategic Planning Program, a project that involves action teams working out specific plans for change, setting philosophy and goals, and presenting them to the school board.

LEARN, the The Los Angeles Educational Alliance for Restructuring Now, is another example of parents taking a major role in deciding their children's education.

Across the country, parents who want to be heard, who want to take their schools back, who want to feel connected to their children's schools, are joining together to enable the schools to become more effective. They hope to foster a climate of greater understanding and cooperation in which new instructional and motivational programs can be developed and improve learning.

## VOUCHER CONCEPT

Another political proposal being discussed today is the voucher system. The voucher allows parents to apply the money that would have been spent on a public school education in their community to a private school of their choice.

## SUMMING UP...

Multiple choices of schools exist throughout America. Whether you and your child decide to participate in one of the new community-based programs or choose to go with one of the more traditional routes, you can feel very good about the likelihood of finding an appropriate school for your family in today's educational climate.

Why not take a moment to review the types of school discussed in this chapter and consider once more how your child will respond to each? You might want to rank the top two or three choices from your point of view and from your child's point of view. Do you disagree with each other? Are there any surprises?

Perhaps the next chapter will help resolve your doubts...or affirm what you already believe to be the best choice. Our charts make use of the numbers assigned to each type of school in this chapter. These charts may make it easier for you to match your child's personality with the type of school that will be most likely to challenge and satisfy both of you.

## CHAPTER 3

# LEARNING ABOUT
# YOUR CHILD'S SCHOOL NEEDS

At first, it may seem odd that we advise you to take time to *evaluate your own child*, but it is important to stand back and look at your child from a bit of a distance. Even though you see your child every day and watch closely as she grows and changes, you have probably not spent much time focusing solely on your child from the specific perspectives of educational development and emotional needs — as they relate to her optimum school choice.

This chapter is designed to help you assess not only your child, but also yourself and your family before determining which school is right for all of you.

## FAMILY STYLE AND SCHOOL STYLE

### Academics Only

Some schools concentrate on academics and address only those socialization skills that are necessary for academic learning. They do not, for example, provide religious training, morality training, sex education, or other non-academic activities as part of the curriculum.

If you and your family have a strong sense of how these non-academic components should be taught and instilled in your child, and if you really are able to take the time to deal with these issues at home, you may decide that an academics-only school will be most appropriate.

## Socialization and Morality Training

Other families expect socialization and morality training to be universal — that is, addressed both at home and at school. Solely academic schools will not meet that objective, of course, but even other types of schools may be found wanting, if your expectations are too high.

Indeed, families who believe that all moral and religious training should occur in the school are likely to discover that the family's involvement cannot be fully replaced in any school environment.

If the school's non-academic teachings are incompatible with your family's views and teachings, the result can be stress and conflict for your child.

## Matching School Structure with Family Structure

The customary, but not always correct, approach is to find a school that treats structure in the same manner as your family does. For example, a loosely structured family may well find that their child adapts quickly to the loosely structured go-at-your-own-pace school we described in Chapter 2. By the same token, the highly structured family may find that their child quickly adapts to the rigidly structured, accelerated academic school program.

But there are *important exceptions*.

For example, a child may not be sufficiently challenged at a school which is too similar to the family style. If he comes from a loosely-structured family but enrolls in a go-at-your-own-pace school, he may find that his academic progress is not adequately encouraged. He may need a more structured school environment in order to learn and to develop important coping skills.

Similarly, the child from the highly-structured family may learn new skills by attending and succeeding in the loosely-structured school environment. In both of these cases, the child may increase self-esteem by learning to succeed in both types of environments, one at home and the contrasting style school.

How do you know that your child is strong enough to meet this challenge? Among the many factors you will consider in selecting a school according to style, the touchstone is often the psychological strength and self-assurance of your child. If your child exhibits psychological balance and strength, your child may be a good candidate to succeed in a school that is the opposite style from your home environment.  If your child lacks self-assurance, your child would be at higher risk in the opposite style school environment.

## WHAT IS YOUR FAMILY'S STYLE?

You are *loosely* structured, if you tend to

- ❑ Do things as needed.
- ❑ Take care of things as they come along.
- ❑ Tend to respond to the needs of the moment.

You are *highly* structured, if you tend to

- ❑ Have many rituals and rules.  For example, you generally schedule your meals at the same time each day.
- ❑ Involve yourselves in recreational activities in precise patterns.
- ❑ Repeat your Sunday afternoon rituals weekly.

## DESCRIBE YOUR FAMILY STYLE

Take a moment to write about your style at home in the space provided below.  Which of the descriptions listed above sound familiar?  As in a kind of "weather report", describe the prevailing climate at home.  Does the family watch television in shared silence, or do you often have conversations together?  Do you sit down together for meals, or do the kids eat at the kitchen table while Mom cleans up?

Our family style:_____

_____

_____

_____

_____

## FAMILY LEGACY

One factor in your family's style is any educational legacy you might share — for example, a tradition that all of the sons go to military school.  Unfortunately, some families virtually force their child to go to a school that is inappropriate, without questioning the family legacy.

Of course, the advantages to having a legacy are very strong: everyone knows you or your family, the interview will undoubtedly go easier, your child will already be familiar with many aspects of the school, she and the family will have much to talk about through her years there. But sometimes, no matter how convenient it is, legacy might not be enough of a reason to choose a school if that school might be wrong for a particular child.

**CASE STUDY:** Everybody in the family had gone to UCLA, but Michael, showing normals signs of adolescence, was letting his high school grades slip because of his sudden interest in politics and school government.

His parents, panicked that he might be throwing away his chance of acceptance to the traditional family alma mater, came to us for help. We suggested that everyone relax, because he showed us that he had the proper attitude about his studies, his future and the family goal of UCLA, but needed a short break from the intensity of studies to expand into other areas. We created a way to balance all of these competing interests to everyone's satisfaction. He was accepted into UCLA, where he is doing well.

## UNDERSTANDING YOUR CHILD

Knowing your child's needs, strengths and weaknesses facilitates finding and evaluating schools — not in terms of which school is absolutely better than another school, but which is best for your child. Your search will be most successful when you keep in mind just how he is unique and different from all other children.

Think for a moment about your child's personality.

Is your son outgoing, or does he have trouble making new friends? How well does he respond to any new situations? Remember, some schools will be more likely to serve the children in your immediate neighborhood than the community at large. Very likely, most of your son's friends will be attending the same school. If you feel strongly that this school is educationally inferior to the private school in another community, think about the effect on your child's social life of transferring him. Spending the school day away from his neighborhood playmates can result in social isolation, if not ostracism. Your child will be seen as different.

Some children can handle this situation much better than others. If they are more socially outgoing and their self-esteem is high, they will be able to balance the somewhat disjointed social life created by living in one community and going to school in another area. If not, there can be emotional repercussions.

Another point to consider is how this will impact on you. Especially with a young child or pre-adolescent, it will be your responsibility to help balance your child's social life. If your daughter's school chums live across town, be prepared to do a lot of driving. Whether your choice is public or private school, social contact with school friends is vital to your child's well being.

Another area to consider is how well your child does in an academically aggressive environment. If your daughter thrives on competition, great. If she is withdrawn and has difficulty asserting herself in group situations, then you should consider this aspect of her personality when you evaluate the schools available to you.

The bottom line is finding the school that will best meet your child's academic and emotional needs. Since the person most directly affected by your choice is your child, remember to *get your son's or daughter's input* before you settle on either the public or private sector. Talk about the schools you are considering and find out what your child's preference is. You might be surprised at what you find out.

Your assessment of your child and your family will lead to general conclusions about the needs of your child in *three basic areas*:

1.    How much structure does my child need? _____
      _____

2.    What size class does my child need? _____
      _____

3.    What learning style does my child prefer? _____
      _____

Before we look at those areas in more detail, take a moment to write down a general description of your child, looking at him primarily in his role as a student going to a new school. (This exercise will help you organize your thoughts for other aspects of the school selection process, such as preparing for your interview with admissions officials.)

What my child is like:_____

_____

_____

_____

_____

_____

_____

## LEARNING STYLES

One misconception perpetuated in education today is that the typical classroom should have a homogeneous group of students. This is simply not true. An effective classroom must accommodate different learning styles.

This *variety of learning styles* occurs not only in the classroom but throughout society. People respond through different channels as ways to learn.

The most dominant individual learning styles are auditory, visual, and kinesthetic. You don't have to be an expert to determine which one(s) your child uses.

*Auditory learners* want to hear information, then intuit the answer. They are especially likely to pick up on verbal *faux pas*. Poets are generally auditory learners.

*Visual learners* become impatient and overloaded in their studying unless they have visual aides or cues to assist them. They also create their own visual aides as they absorb ideas, creating them in their minds. Mathematicians are likely to be visual learners.

*Kinesthetic learners* learn by doing. Put in simplest terms, they learn by using their bodies. They see something happen, then they learn by imitating what they have just seen. Athletes usually learn in this way. Kinesthetic learning is the primary system infants and children use.

Kinesthetic learners would agree with the old Chinese proverb: I hear and I forget; I see and I remember; I do and I understand.

A few simple questions will help you determine whether your child is primarily an auditory or a visual learner: Does your child make notes to help him or her remember things, or does your child tend just to store new information in his or her memory after hearing it?  Does your child feel a need to touch things or participate actively rather than just watch in order to learn?

When auditory learners hear another person say, "I'll be there at 8 o'clock," they understand the meaning as "between 7:45 and 8:15."  Visual learners expect to be met at 8 o'clock sharp.  They are upset or surprised when the person is "late".

Actually, the *integration of all the styles* promotes the best understanding and learning.  The most effective teachers — like the most effective speakers in all areas of life — are those whose presentations include all three modes.

## MY CHILD AS A LEARNER

For more of an in-depth assessment of your child as learner, spend some time with the following questions.

There are no "correct" answers for this exercise; there is no score.  Instead, these questions are meant to help you consider various aspects of your child's uniqueness and needs that you might not otherwise have thought about.

My child tends to ...

❑    learn at different rates in different areas

❑    learn slowly in a number of areas

❑    need individual teaching

❑    need to be physically involved with learning activities rather than to learn only by reading and listening

❑    be highly creative and imaginative

❑    be generally a self-starter

Now consider some specific *alternatives* as you assess your child's learning style:

1.  ❏  Does my child need a small classroom to be drawn out to partici-
       pate?

    *or*

    ❏  Does my child need a larger classroom in order to have many social
       choices and not be able to monopolize the classroom?

2.  ❏  Does my child need a fast-paced education program to avoid being
       bored?

    *or*

    ❏  Does my child need a fundamental education process that includes
       regular repetition and reinforcement in order to retain learning?

3.  ❏  Does my child respond or perform best when there are quickly-paced
       activities that demand quickly-paced responses?

    *or*

    ❏  Does my child respond or perform best when there is no time pres-
       sure?

4.  ❏  Does my child need to be at the higher level of the class average in
       order to avoid feelings of inadequacy?

    *or*

    ❏  Does my child need to be in a class where the majority of the class
       perform at a higher level in order to encourage my child to increase
       performance?

5.   ❏   Does my child primarily learn visually (reading and observing)?

     *or*

     ❏   Does my child primarily learn auditorily (discussions and listening)?

     *or*

     ❏   Does my child primarily learn kinesthetically (physical activities and creating tangible projects for learning)?

6.   ❏   Does my child need a school that emphasizes my child's aptitudes?

     *or*

     ❏   Does my child need a school that will emphasize other areas for balance?

Now think about your response to the following *general questions about your child's needs in school...*

Does my child do best in highly structured settings or function well independently?

Does my child do better with challenges and will get bored if not stimulated enough?

Does my child adore group projects or seek solitary projects?

Does my child separate easily, wake up asking expectantly: "Is this a school day?"

Will my child be left out because a school is so far geographically that it discourages developing relationships?

Does my child have any learning disabilities?

Does my child have learning delays?

Does my child have any physical limitations?

Should my child receive religious training at the school?

Is my child closely attached to friends or siblings who already have made a school selection?

Does my child structure activities independently or wait for another person to plan the activity?

Now, write down any of your child's significant attributes that are not included above, considering how they relate to the best potential school choice:

_____
_____
_____
_____
_____
_____

Continuing your evaluation of your child's unique personality and needs, review the following list of activities and abilities and think about them in relation to the types of school you will be considering.

**My Child's Preferred Style(s) of Play:**

❑ outdoor play?
❑ indoor play?
❑ solitary play?
❑ playing with siblings only?
❑ playing with other children?
❑ playing with siblings and other children?
❑ playing with only one peer at a time?
❑ playing with two or three at a time?
❑ other types of play unique to my child are: _____
_____
_____
_____
_____
_____
_____

**My Child's Preferred Activities:**

❑   intricate art projects, sports, watching TV, computer games, music, indoor play, drawing?

❑   activities my child dislikes or avoids?

❑   favorite things to do inside?

❑   favorite things to do outside?

❑   favorite entertainment? (Plays, symphony, movies, video games, etc.)

❑   prefers imaginative forms of play, such as dressing up, playing house, playing school, playing with dolls or stuffed animals?

❑   prefers passive activities, such as watching television, watching sports, playing video games, or going to movies?

## MATCHING YOUR CHILD AND SCHOOL

### Our Self-Help Questionnaire

Choose the words from the following list to describe your child. If you have a lot of "A" responses, your child is likely to need more structure; if you have a lot of "B" responses, your child is likely to need a smaller, more freely structured classroom.

The numbers following each category refer to the nine types of schools described in Chapter 2. The order that the numbers appear in is preferential; the numbers that appear first might be the best type of school to consider first.

For example, if you would describe your child as "shy," we find that he would do well in all types of schools, except for the loosely structured ones (8). If you think that he is "impulsive," he will probably not do well in any type of school except middle-of-the-road (5). If you know that he seeks out group projects instead of choosing to work alone, three choices seem preferable to us: move-at-your-own pace (2) comes first, followed by loosely structured (8) and then special talent (4).

Please understand that these are guidelines that attempt to balance quite a few general factors, based upon the unlikely circumstance that all nine types of schools are equally available to you. Your final decision will be the result of weighing pluses and minuses in terms of your child's and your family's characteristics and needs.

To refresh your memory, these are the nine types of schools:

1. Highly accelerated
2. Move-at-your-own-pace
3. Traditional
4. Special talent
5. Middle-of-the-road
6. Religious
7. Highly structured, highly disciplined
8. Loosely structured
9. College prep

Responds well to *structure* (A):

- ❑ Shy - all except 8
- ❑ Impulsive - 5
- ❑ Overactive - 2, 3, 5
- ❑ A leader - 2, 3, 5
- ❑ Prefers to play with others - 2, 8, 1, 3, 7, 9
- ❑ Needs to be entertained all the time - 3, 7, 9, 5
- ❑ Seeks group projects - 2, 8, 4
- ❑ Needs extra time to learn - 2, 8
- ❑ Avoids challenges - 2, 8, 4, 5
- ❑ Scientific - 4, 7, 1, 9, 3, 5
- ❑ Athletic - 3, 5, 7, 9
- ❑ Dependent - 7, 3, 5, 9
- ❑ Clingy - 7, 3, 5
- ❑ Has only one or two special friends - 8, 2, 4, 5
- ❑ Has no friends - 2, 8, 7, 5, 3
- ❑ Mathematical - 7, 1, 3, 5, 9
- ❑ Writing and Language - 8, 2, 5, 3, 7, 9
- ❑ Public or social service - 8, 2, 6
- ❑ Socially immature - 7, 1, 3, 5, 9
- ❑ Competitive - 7, 1, 3, 5, 9

*Freer-form* curriculum (B):

- ❏ Slow to warm up - 7, 3, 5, 4, 9
- ❏ Passive - 7, 5, 3, 6
- ❏ Inventive - 8, 2, 4
- ❏ A follower - 5, 7, 3, 6
- ❏ Prefers to play alone - 8, 2
- ❏ Likes quiet time - 8, 2, 4
- ❏ Seeks solitary projects - 8, 2, 4
- ❏ Seeks challenges - 8, 2, 1, 9
- ❏ Musical - 4, 3, 7, 1, 9
- ❏ Artistic - 4, 8, 2
- ❏ Independent - 8, 2, 1
- ❏ Manual Arts - 5, 7, 4
- ❏ Socially advanced - 8, 2, 1, 3, 4, 5, 6, 7, 9
- ❏ Non-competitive - 8, 2, 4, 5, 6, 7

*Both* A and B:

- ❏ Outgoing - 8, 2, 4, 1, 3, 6, 9
- ❏ Quick to learn - 1, 2, 4, 8, 7, 9
- ❏ Has many friends - 7, 3, 5, 6, 9

## IS YOUR VERY YOUNG CHILD READY FOR SCHOOL?

If you are evaluating a preschooler, several important considerations will affect your choice. In the first place, you want to be sure that your child is actually ready to take this important step.

Many parents come to us for help in deciding whether or not their children are ready to attend kindergarten. We begin with the *child's age*: many private schools require that an applicant be 5 years old by October 1, some have a September 1 cut-off date. Several schools have different cut-off dates according to sex: September 1 for girls, June 1 for boys. For public schools the traditional cut-off date is the first of September.

How important is your child's *age in comparison with his classmates*? In recent studies, experts have found that older students have an advantage in a classroom, particularly socially and particularly in adolescence. Indeed, there is evidence suggesting that the older students may have a lower risk for such emotional problems as depression and drug use.

After considering the age question, you will want to have your pediatrician screen your child's vision and hearing:

1.   The *visual check* should include all of the following:

   • color blindness
   • visual field
   • near and far vision
   • ability to accommodate from near to far and back again
   • visual perceptual skills (figure on ground, etc.)
   • how close or far does the child hold paper or book

**NOTE:** Color blindness is sometimes easily overlooked. When one kindergarten boy was drawing grass, an adult commented, "Gee, it's interesting that you chose that shade of gray for the grass." She thought the color was part of the artistic interpretation. It wasn't.

2.   The *auditory screening* should be complete, including a check of your child's ability to discriminate between sounds.

   Even when her hearing is acute, she may lack the ability to make subtle discriminations: for example, between b and d, or p and g. 90% of what we ask children to do in education requires auditory discrimination ability.

## CAN MY CHILD CONCENTRATE WELL ENOUGH?

Even at the kindergarten level, there is a strong emphasis on *attention and concentration ability*. It is difficult to sort out whether a young wiggly child who can't sit still is simply a bit too young for kindergarten or has some of the attributes of Attention Deficit Disorder. It may be age-appropriate for your child to have some inattention problems, but if the degree of inattentiveness and "wiggliness" is severe enough, you might want to have your child evaluated by a psychologist, pediatric neurologist, or pediatrician before he starts school.

Research shows that the child who can sit still and listen will do fine in school. In fact, this ability overrides cultural and language issues.

Yet many of our children are struggling with what we consider the basic behaviors required for participation in kindergarten. If your child isn't sitting still and paying attention, she no longer looks like a student. Being informed about the attitudes and attributes of your child's readiness for kindergarten will help make decisions regarding placement.

Keep in mind that different schools have different attitudes toward the kind of behavior they think appropriate. When one of the authors was asked to visit a kindergarten to evaluate a child with supposed attention problems, she was horrified to find that the child's crimes were wiggling and sitting on his knees. In another type of preschool setting, there would have been no cause for concern.

**FOUR YEAR OLD READINESS TEST**

This is a test you can try at home.

1.  Give one command at a time. For example, you might say, "Please, Amy, go to the bedroom and bring me the pink hairbrush."

2.  When you find she can follow one step, ask her to follow a two-step command. Emphasize the words "first" and "then." For example, you might say, "Amy, would you first bring me the pink hairbrush, and then bring me the yellow key ring."

3.  Finally, see if your child can follow three steps in sequence. This simple test has become the most reliable predictor of kindergarten success: Your child's ability to follow three oral commands in sequence.

## OTHER FACTORS FOR YOU TO CONSIDER

Many other variables need to be considered when you are choosing whether to advance a child into kindergarten or hold him back a year:

• the size of the child

• physical stamina

• ability to go without a nap

- peer and social skills

- likes being with other children (at times, not necessarily all the time)

- ability to tolerate a longer day

- language development (The key is comprehension more than expression. Can your child comprehend directions and information?)

- emotional development (When we look at very bright children who can do all tasks but are socially and/or emotionally less developed, we recommend you wait because the academic talent will continue to develop and the child can be supplemented with an enrichment program the next year.)

- tolerance for the new, flexibility.

## BASIC QUESTIONS TO ASK YOURSELF

How does my child handle transition between home and other places? What are his expectations about kindergarten? Will he be able to handle the school's policy about separation and transition?

Does my child separate easily? Will he wake up asking expectantly, "Is this a school day?"

Are you ready to make this transition? If YOU are not, your child won't be, either.

## READINESS CHECKLIST

A change is occurring in the requirements for children in kindergarten. They are more like what used to be expected of entering first-graders. At some schools, your child may be expected to know the alphabet, colors and shapes, in addition to directional and positional skills (over, under, left, right).

Kindergartens vary across America, but we suggest that you use this checklist as a benchmark of what to look for in a kindergarten-aged child. Then ask the schools you are considering what they expect as readiness skills.

**BASIC SCHOOL READINESS SKILLS:**

❏   Naming colors

❏   Matching colors

❏   Counting to 10, possibly 20

❏   Some number recognition

❏   Some size perception; for example, recognizing bigger vs. smaller

❏   Join sets of objects

❏   Matching shapes

❏   Copying shapes; for example, the ability to approximate a square or a cross (crossed lines)

❏   Knowing body parts

❏   Knowing such personal information as full name, parents' names, address, telephone number, birthday

❏   Able to play cooperatively, at least to some degree

❏   Ability to listen to a story and participate in discussing it.

❏   Ability to recognize likenesses and differences; that is, are two things the same or different?

❏   Ability to identify patterns; for example, look at a group of objects and identify which one(s) belong and which one(s) don't.

❏   Can say or sing the alphabet. Letter recognition is optimal.

❏   Has such self-help skills as being able to put on clothing, tie and button, and put shoe on the proper foot.

❏   Is independent with toilet needs—flushing, wiping, redressing.

As you complete your evaluation of your child, you may find that you would be well advised to consider some of the following concepts: developmental kindergarten, retention, special education, and professional evaluation.

## DEVELOPMENTAL KINDERGARTEN

"Developmental kindergarten", a relatively recent concept in preschool education, offers a little bit of both preschool and kindergarten. It acts as a bridge between a non-academic play-preschool environment and an academic kindergarten environment.

In short, what your child will get in a developmental kindergarten is more play than in a standard kindergarten and more academics than in a standard preschool. The contrast with a traditional kindergarten is something like the difference between Mr. Rogers and Sesame Street. Like a developmental program, Mr. Rogers moves in real time using a combination of fantasy and realism. Sesame Street is more of a quickly-paced information-type program.

It is common for *kindergarten programs to be more accelerated today* than in the past. Some even have children ready to read by mid-year. This can be a disadvantage for a child who is kindergarten-ready but not as academically advanced as necessary for an accelerated program. This child might do better in a developmental kindergarten.

The developmental kindergarten concept has proved successful in many schools, especially with children who are not quite ready for kindergarten because emotionally and socially they need more play, while at the same time their curiosity and eagerness to learn causes them to be restless and sometimes act out from boredom. A developmental kindergarten provides both a more stimulating environment and opportunities for social and emotional development.

## RETENTION

A school may raise the question of whether to accelerate your child to a new grade or retain him in the same grade for a repeat year. Many factors come into play in making this decision, factors which require careful, thorough evaluation.

**What are the Reasons for Retention?**

❑ Speech and language delays

❑ Learning disability needs

❑ Place in family (for example, acceleration or retention will cause two siblings to be in the same grade)

❑ Need to repeat a grade in order to improve skills

**What are the Questions to Ask?**

❑ Is my child especially mature for her age?

❑ Is my child especially immature for his age?

❑ Is my child a leader, or a follower?

❑ Does my child prefer younger friends, or older friends?

❑ Is my child passive, or aggressive?

Parents are often concerned that retention will result in their child's being bored by having to repeat information he's already studied. In fact, it will often be presented in a slightly different form, allowing your child to feel on top of the information rather than bored.

If you decide to retain your child, keep in mind that it works better sooner rather than later, preferably in kindergarten or in the first grade. Otherwise, you may lose more than you could hope to gain. At the kindergarten level, repetition can be very positive.

Once a decision to retain is made, parents need to be in full agreement to avoid further conflict for the child and in the child.

Be flexible, and be prepared to be your child's best advocate. If you notice that she can handle kindergarten only from 9:00 A.M. to 11:30 A.M. and then loses interest or is exhausted, pick her up early and let her rest. Maybe this will be necessary for just a month, but it can make all the difference in the long run.

## CHOOSING A SCHOOL FOR A SPECIAL EDUCATION CHILD

If your child is a special education child, your best option may be in the public school system, where resources are often excellent. To take advantage of these public school services, the first step is to become informed about exactly what programs are available to serve your child's special needs.

You and your child have a right to enjoy the benefits of these programs. The school principal or psychologist will provide you with a fact sheet that describes your rights as the parent of a special education child, as well as the procedure for a fair hearing if you believe that your child is not receiving the appropriate services.

Non-public school funding is money provided by the local school district to pay for a child to go to another school that would have a more appropriate setting for that child's needs. Funds are limited at this point because of the dramatic fiscal crisis in many public school systems.

## WHEN PROFESSIONAL EVALUATION MAY BE NECESSARY

Should you seek an independent evaluation of your child by a professional?
We don't think such evaluations are necessary unless you have serious concerns about when to start your child's formal education, or about your child's academic, social, or emotional progress.

The advantage of doing an evaluation is to identify strengths and weaknesses, to determine the best possible academic plan, to understand different learning styles, and to come up with strategies for raising a child's self-esteem.

If you are concerned that your child is gifted and qualifies for special enrichment services, you might ask for an evaluation by the school psychologist. If the school cannot provide testing, ask if they will accept testing from other professionals.

## CHAPTER 4

# EVALUATING THE SCHOOL

## EIGHT BASIC AREAS FOR YOUR LONG-TERM PLANNING

Now that you have decided what general types of schools to consider for your child, this chapter will give you some more in-depth ways by which to evaluate the schools.

We begin with a good general rule: When you choose an elementary school or a secondary school for your child, you have to strike a balance between two different but complementary points of view.

On the one hand, the right school is the one that will *best serve your child's immediate needs* and enrich her academic, social and personal lives today. On the other, it must be *appropriate for the long term*, because her formal education will probably include college — and perhaps graduate or professional school.

Keeping both perspectives always in mind, you should assess the schools you are considering in light of the *eight areas* of emphasis we discuss throughout this chapter. In Chapter Five, we provide SCHOOL EVALUATION FORMS for you to use on visits to schools that interest you. They are a convenient, succinct tool for keeping a record of what you discover in these eight basic areas.

**REMINDER:** As we have stressed in previous chapters, the best school is the one that most completely suits the needs, interests and goals of your child. Be sure to distinguish, therefore, between the school that is the most prestigious in the community and the one that is really going to make that nearly perfect match.

## EIGHT BASIC AREAS TO CONSIDER IN SCHOOL EVALUATIONS

1.  Academic curricula

2.  School's educational philosophy

3.  Teachers and other staff

4.  Class size

5.  Students

6.  Any special characteristics, including religious affiliation or subject area concentration, like arts or science

7.  Parental involvement: the opportunities, the expectations

8.  Physical facilities

Each of these topics is discussed in detail below.

As you investigate them for yourself, **don't just listen to friends and neighbors**, or to your daughter's peers. Their enthusiasms can be very seductive but will not necessarily answer to your child's needs. Quite understandably, too, your friends may have an agenda of wanting you involved with them. Listen to them, of course, because they will see things differently from school officials, but don't let their opinions substitute for your own work of evaluating.

**Be leery of the open house for prospective students.** This can also be dangerously seductive. School staff will be putting their best foot forward, as they should, but their planned program may distract you from finding out the specific information that concerns you and your child. In addition, this tends to be a social occasion, and you do not want to make a nuisance of yourself by monopolizing a teacher's or school official's time. Courteously ask for an appointment for your evaluation visit and save your probing questions until then.

## 1. ACADEMIC CURRICULA

The following questions should help you direct your thinking in this first area:

What is the primary teaching style?  In other words, is most teaching by lecture, or do workbooks and written projects play a large role in learning?  Are there assignment books?  Are there physical learning activities which are integrated into the  teaching?

At what grade does homework begin?  What is the level of homework?

Are the courses coordinated from one year to the next?  Are the courses age-appropriate?  Do children from several different years take the same classes together?  Is there cross-age tutoring?  Are the children encouraged to assist each other in learning?  Are independent study programs offered?

Do the courses include foreign language, science, horticulture, art, music, theater arts, dance, computers, library use, cross-cultural experiences, community service, ethics, government, and religion?

**POSITIVE ATTITUDE HINT:**  The answers to these questions will not necessarily be positive or negative in themselves.  For example, whether or not "cross-age tutoring" is a good thing will depend upon the needs, skills and attitudes of your child.

Consider that the child who is bright, extroverted and self-starting does best in a varied program that includes a large number of enrichment classes.  By   contrast, the child who needs organization and repetition to solidify his learning will usually do better with a curriculum that is highly structured around a core group of courses and subjects.  And the child who is interested in music, art or other non-academic subjects does best in a school with a curriculum and facilities that emphasize these areas.

## SPECIFIC THINGS TO LOOK FOR

On your tour of the school, you will probably encounter a display of textbooks and other items that help illustrate the curriculum.  This is a perfect starting-point for taking your in-depth look at the school's program, aims, and methods of instruction.

*Examine the textbooks.* Are they appropriate for your child? Ask why these particular books are being used. How often are they reviewed and changed? Do they follow your state's recommended guidelines? Are the textbooks age-appropriate? In other words, do seventh graders have to struggle through college textbooks, or twelfth graders make do with seventh grade material?

*Read through the total curriculum.* You want to understand the progression of learning that your child might experience throughout her years at this school. Are the classes segregated by age or by academic standing? Are all the basics covered (English, mathematics, history, science, etc.)? What is the balance between academic subjects and enrichment subjects?

*Are study skills taught?* Traditionally not taught until high school or college, study skills are increasingly addressed at lower levels. Is the school's study skills class (if it offers one) given separately or integrated into some other class such as English or history? If there is not a special class in study skills, do teachers take the time to address the issue with students? Does your child need this help?

*Ask to see a typical test and/or homework assignment* so you can determine what level of work will be required. Do the requirements strike you as excessively difficult and lengthy, or are they fair and appropriate? Ask how often tests are given. If your child is adept at taking tests, he'll do fine at a school that relies upon frequent quizzes. If your child frazzles under pressure, then look for a school that emphasizes projects over tests.

*What about day-to-day pressures?* Are long hours devoted to classwork with only brief recesses? Are children encouraged to compete too vigorously with each other? Will weekend assignments become a burden to your child? Will she be bored if competition is discouraged?

**CASE STUDY:** One client was horrified to discover that her seventh grade daughter's textbooks were primarily at the college level. What happened to being twelve and in the seventh grade she wondered? Her daughter Jessica said, "Now my life is getting up, going to school, coming home, doing homework and falling exhausted into bed, only to know that the next day I'll be doing the same thing all over again." Her mother is disappointed with herself for not doing enough to protect Jessica by making a thorough review of the school and its academic demands. This shock added damaging stress just when both parent and child needed to be focusing their energies on getting accustomed to a new environment.

## 2. SCHOOL'S EDUCATIONAL PHILOSOPHY

Be aware of the possibility of a HIDDEN CURRICULUM.

Occasionally, a school might claim to teach in one way but actually provide a very different kind of instruction. We are not necessarily talking about some sinister aspect of school life. Whether consciously or not, the faculty and staff will probably do their work in light of the school's underlying philosophy. Each school has one. Different ideas or ways of learning become important in different schools. Teachers, too, do not work in a vacuum. Their teaching is necessarily a reflection of their beliefs and values.

Probably, the school will make available written statements about its goals — for example, development of character, stress upon foundational academic subjects, encouragement of socialization. But do they really pursue the aims they advertise?

*The implementation of hidden curricula may be as important as or more important than the course topic.* Is history being taught in order to impart a particular view of morals? Is science being taught as a means of training students to memorize facts or accept information unquestioningly? Is sex education being taught in order to present or challenge religious beliefs? Is the emphasis on learning the subject matter, or on learning how to think and analyze?

If you rely solely on the promotional brochure or list of courses, you may learn little more than the names of various classes at the different grade levels. Visiting the school, walking through the classrooms and completing the school evaluation forms will usually provide enough information about the hidden curriculum if you are looking for it.

To repeat, the hidden curriculum is the school's motivating philosophy — not necessarily bad or good in itself — and you want to *decide for yourself whether or not it matches or complements your philosophy*.

### SPECIFIC AIMS OF SCHOOL PHILOSOPHY:

Most commonly, four aims are considered of bedrock importance by most schools today:

1.  Teach academic subjects

2.   Foster your child's social and emotional well-being

3.   Teach a religious or moral view, and

4.   Teach a socioethical "citizen of the world" viewpoint

Given these generally shared aims, however, you need to determine how much emphasis a school places on each in relation to the other three.

You can find that out by checking the following *markers of school philosophy*:

1.   Curriculum

2.   Faculty

3.   Expectations about parental involvement, and

4.   Types of families and students selected by the school

For example, some schools believe that their primary charge is to ensure that each student learns in a prescribed manner.  The student takes a set of core courses, acquires a set of study skills, and masters a set of test-taking skills.  The school's goal is to encourage the child's ability to perform academically so that she can be accepted at prestigious educational institutions of higher learning.

By contrast, other schools believe that their primary charge is to cultivate the individual interests and abilities of each student, to let him learn at his own pace, and to guide him in developing as his own nature directs from within.

The former approach, if not appropriate for your child, may cause her to experience stress, suffer from psychological problems and fail to develop her social skills.  The latter approach, if not a match for your child, could result in inflated, false sense of achievement.  Therefore, *knowing the philosophy of the school increases the chances that the school selected will be the best for your child*.

## HOW TO CLARIFY YOUR OWN PHILOSOPHY

The family looking for a highly accelerated academic program should not waste time, energy and money exploring such low-key developmental programs as "move-at-your-own-pace" type of schools. By the same token, you have no reason to visit an accelerated college prep program that stresses rigorous testing when you have a child who is well-rounded, benefits from age-appropriate instruction and needs a curriculum that emphasizes creative and critical thought.

**CASE STUDY:** Zoe is unhappy at her new school, she explains, "because at this school, there is always a right way or a wrong way to do something, but at my old school there were many ways to do it. I just memorize now. They are not asking me to think the information through." Accustomed to learning biology in hands-on experiments, Zoe was disappointed to find that her new chemistry class stresses textbook memorization over direct involvement.

At her new school, a current presidential election was studied as a historical process. Former classmates at her previous school told Zoe that they were being asked to think critically about the issues and candidates and were being given assignments focused on the current events and issues of the election.

Unfortunately, she and her parents had not evaluated her new school's philosophy before she transferred.

Before you start the application process, you need to identify just *what type of school you want your child to attend*. In most cities there will be a large variety of potential schools to choose from.

We are not talking about superior and mediocre, but about finding schools that match your child's social, emotional and academic needs. What may be a questionable choice for you may be just the right placement for your friend or another child.

**CASE STUDIES:** We know one school that is so focused on creativity they completely disregard grammar and punctuation. When Mark transferred from there to a more demanding school, he was virtually traumatized by the shock of discovering how poor his basic skills seemed in comparison with his new classmates. Since both of his parents had done well in traditional academic schools, they had not foreseen his shock and dismay.

False feedback can be the result when a school's philosophy makes it overly protective of a child's self-esteem. You may be pleased with this approach, but should recognize the possible consequences. For example, Rita received glowing anecdotal teacher reports during her years at elementary school. When she applied to a competitive middle school her actual academic skills were too weak for her to be considered. When she and her mother came to us for evaluation, we discovered that it took Rita four hours to do homework that should have taken an hour. The school left it to us to be their messenger about her actual progress.

What if your child needs one learning environment, but you are more comfortable with another? Some children can tolerate noise, clutter, and lots of movement in the classroom. If you are appalled by this kind of situation, learn how to recognize that what your child needs can be quite different from what you would want.

Or perhaps your child matches a college prep school, but you would have been happier at his age in a go-at-your-own-pace school. To repeat, he is the one experiencing the school, not you.

## A GUIDE TO IDENTIFYING YOUR PHILOSOPHY

What is your concept of the ideal school for your particular child?

How closely does each school approach that ideal?

Are you looking for a school that offers creative projects and lots of art and music, or would you prefer an emphasis on fundamentals like basic grammar, mathematics, science, computer knowledge and so forth?

Do required school uniforms cause your heart to swell with pride or frighten you as emblems of conformity?

Do you demand a school with green lawns and playgrounds or can you tolerate a less picturesque place that offers exciting education for your child?

Do you want religious training as part of the school day or only a secular experience? Can you tolerate secular education that uses church or temple grounds?

Do you prefer morals and values education to be part of the curriculum or left to the home?

Do you prefer sex education and human development courses taught as part of the curriculum or only at home? Are you comfortable with the methods used to teach these subjects? Who devised the curriculum? Can your child be excused from aspects that are not part of your philosophy and beliefs?

Will your child be able to handle the complexities of entering a school that is culturally different from your home environment: for example, going from a working class neighborhood into an upper class school?

Does the school provide curriculum modifications and flexibility?

Does the school's approach to discipline seem reasonable and productive to you?

Does the staff know how to respond if your child feels excluded from the in group?

**CASE STUDY:** We have seen children as young as seven year old Marilyn distraught at not being like the other children. She said, "I speak another language from theirs." She plays violin and her family listens to classical music. When the movie *Batman* was the talk of the school, she wasn't interested, couldn't talk about seeing it and felt left out.

Schools have a responsibility in this area. How they handle such problems can have a powerful, lasting influence on children in their ability to integrate into social groups and yet remain unique in their individuality. Schools need to realize how lifelong and how painful these scars of social exclusion can be.

## SCHOOL DROP-OUT AND EXPULSION POLICY

A very significant part of a school's philosophy is the *official attitude toward retaining students*. Is the school committed to seeing your child through academic or personal difficulties? Will teachers "go the extra mile", or is the student expected to meet certain standards in order to avoid expulsion? Is the "drop-out" encouraged to come back?

Some schools do their best to retain all students who want to continue through high school graduation, even if they transfer to related or cooperating feeder schools.

But some schools are willing to drop a child who is marginally difficult or for some reason not entirely acceptable to the school community.

If your child has the potential of only marginally satisfactory school performance, choosing a school that believes in an inclusionary and continuation policy may save her from the psychological and academic stress of an unanticipated and involuntary school change.

## SCHOOL POLICY ON BEHAVIORAL PROBLEMS

What if *your* child has behavior problems?

You should find out exactly how the school feels about her specific behavior problems. What will they tolerate and how do they typically deal with behavior that is considered unacceptable?

How are you brought into the process? Who is the final judge of how to handle the problem? What are the procedures used: for example, warning letters, short-term suspensions, detention?

You can avoid a great deal of misunderstanding and unpleasantness by finding out whether or not your philosophy and the school's are in agreement.

## SIBLING PRIORITY POLICY

Some schools give preference in admission and retention to the younger siblings of current students, but others base such decisions entirely upon the individual ability of the child.

Sibling priority was traditionally automatic in private school. If you had at least one child enrolled, you were assured that all of his other siblings would be accepted thereafter. This practice has been largely abandoned for a number of reasons. For one thing, the number of applicants to private school has increased dramatically. For another, administrators now recognize that one student's success at a school does not guarantee the performance of a sibling. In fact, the younger child can have an experience as miserable as the older child's was positive. Sharing the same family does not necessarily mean sharing the same academic abilities or styles of learning.

You need to look at each of your children — individually — and make placement decisions on the basis of each child's needs.  Once you do, they may wind up at the same school or at two or three different schools.

**CASE STUDY:**  We knew one family who decided to place their oldest child in a liberally-experienced or developmental-style school, when the child was actually best suited for a PSAT-paced academic school.  Why?  Because they thought his two younger siblings would be happier in the experimental environment when the time came.  In fact, these children eventually went elsewhere, because they really needed a more specialized small-class environment.  What must have seemed like sensible family planning proved to be detrimental to the oldest child's best interests.

*The Moral:*  Place your child in the environment that is best for her.

## HANDBOOKS AS A SOURCE OF SCHOOL PHILOSOPHY

Most private schools and many public schools produce handbooks that clearly set down their guiding policies and procedures — in other words, *their working philosophy*.   In fact, these handbooks often provide all or most of the information you need for reviewing the eight categories of school analysis. (Do not confuse with the school brochure, which is used primarily for promotional  purposes.)

Read the handbook carefully in order to learn exactly what effect the school's policies will have upon your child.  For example, if he is susceptible to allergies or other medical problems that require him to stay home occasionally, pay special attention to the *guidelines on absences*.  Are all absences treated alike, or are there special exemptions for medically-caused absences?  Is make-up work allowed?  If so, how is it assigned?

Don't make assumptions based upon the policies at your child's current school.  In California, the state guidelines allow a total of 20 days absence before a child is failed.  But we know at least one private school in the Los Angeles area that allows only 9 days absence.

Handbooks also explain the *requirements for graduation*, which vary widely from school to school. More often than you might think possible, a student enters her senior year without having taken the required number of English or math courses.  Sometimes, you and the school might overlook a requirement — for example, the total number of hours of physical education — that can delay your child's graduation.  Make certain that you understand how many credits are required, how they can be lost, and how they can be reinstated or replaced.

Some schools encourage kids to go to **summer school** when they could bene-fit from remediation in academic subjects.  Will your child respond well to this 12-month school year?  Will he have negative feelings about his abilities rein-forced by this approach?  Perhaps camp or art classes or vacations with relatives would be better for his self-concept.  If the handbook isn't completely clear on the issue, ask the school whether summer classes are considered mandatory or just supplementary to the school year.

## 3. TEACHERS AND OTHER STAFF

Ideally, a school faculty consists of highly trained, credentialed individuals who are as gifted as teachers as they are sensitive to the individual needs of all children.  But let's talk about the real world.

You will know what is strongest about a school's faculty because that is **the quality the school will promote**.  If they praise the credentials of the teachers, then you should observe classes in order to see whether or not this fine academ-ic training translates into perceptive teaching on the firing line.  On the other hand, if the school praises its faculty for good teaching and effective interactions with kids, you should find out about their academic credentials.  As in all other areas of school evaluation, the balance between these two extremes is the balance that you think will work best for your child.

One marker for faculty quality is the **rate of turnover and the experience level** of the teachers.  A school at which the majority of teachers have only one or two years of experience is quite possibly a high-risk situation.  On the other hand, a faculty made up almost entirely of veterans with 30 years experience in the same school may supply a different kind of risk: teaching styles may have become stale and rigid, new and effective discoveries in education may be unknown or disre-garded.

Other things being equal, **the preferred faculty** will include a majority of teachers who have a substantial number of years of teaching experience, many of them at this school, along with younger faculty working their way up the ladder. Do experienced teachers work with their newer colleagues in the same classroom? This is often a successful way of integrating new teachers into a stable faculty.  It allows the new teacher to have a successful year while not compromising your child's learning program.

A *system of faculty support* is important to older teachers, too. While additional years of experience can produce a greater ability to deal with the variations among children, it is still important that each teacher benefit from the support of a master teacher, master trainer, or hands-on administrator. In that way, small problems can be solved before they grow into major complications. Almost any teacher will have some level of problem with one or two students in his class. A sensible school administration will recognize this human reality and have procedures in place to deal with it.

Trained, capable *classroom aides* can also be a valuable addition to your child's learning experience, as long as they are monitored by a trained teacher in order to realize their full potential. This kind of supervision and cooperation is crucial to effective teaching.

A *high turnover rate* — for example, faculty tending to leave after only one or two years on staff — may be a strong indicator of a problem school suffering from instability. Investigate to see if the high turnover reflects faculty dissatisfaction or if this is just circumstantial.

## ACCREDITATION

It is important to know which agencies have accredited the school. Is the school accredited by the State and by National boards? Check the Association of Independent Schools to determine the standing of the school. Find out what licenses the school holds. Check over the credentials of administrators as well as teachers.

The State Board of Education in California gives "blue ribbon certification" to certain public schools. Call or write your State Board of Education (or the corresponding agency in your state) or ask the school itself if it has a blue ribbon certification or some similar distinction.

If you are considering a public school, is it a charter school? If so, it can independently set its curriculum, standards, procedure and philosophy (consistent with State requirements) with an independent governing board rather than the Board of Education. Such a school is likely to be a superior institution.

Has the school been rated in comparison with other schools in your area? Have articles about the school's academic history been written in your area newspapers? Your librarian may help you find very valuable information from official and from informal sources.

## 4. CLASS SIZE

As you know, all children have individual needs. If this were not true, standard classes could be videotaped and a fortune would be saved in the education process.

Still, certain general statements can be made in regard to *optimum class size*. The typical public school class size of 30 or more students usually produces an impaired learning environment. The marker for ideal class size in terms of learning well is 22 or fewer. The marker for a sufficient number so that socialization skills will be learned is a class size of 10 or larger (except in special education circumstances). Therefore, your objective is to find an average class size between 15 and 20.

Many educators believe class size to be *as important as any other single factor in the quality of education*. There is ongoing debate as to whether a larger class size, such as 30 students with two teachers, is equivalent to two individual classes of 15. Still, the majority view today is that the smaller class sizes are preferable; that is, the addition of a second teacher to a larger class does not produce the same benefits.

You should look only at schools where class size is small if your child has some or all of the following characteristics:

- ❑ Introverted
- ❑ Impulsive
- ❑ Slow to warm up
- ❑ Passive

## 5. CLASSMATES

Much of your child's learning will come from her classmates. The teacher may act as a guide to socialization skills, but the other kids create the environment in which your child will gain certain kinds of essential knowledge by interacting with her peers. What she comes to think about herself, how she views the world, what she thinks of other human beings — these concepts are all developed as *children learn from other children*.

You should take care that your child will be going to school with others of similar ability and outlook:

Placing an *underachieving child in a top academic school* with classmates who are able to learn with far greater ease is detrimental to that child. The teacher looks for individual differences in children but still targets the   class to the majority.

Placing an *underachieving child in a school situation with students of similar abilities* usually enhances his self-esteem.  With proper educational assistance, he will progress in a manner consistent with his ability.

Placing the *exceptionally bright child with classmates who perform at a far lower level* often may bore her so much that she develops disruptive behavior, poor socialization skills, and extra difficulties in relating to and with classmates. This is just as inappropriate as placing the underachiever in an accelerated academic program.

## 6. SPECIAL CHARACTERISTICS OF THE SCHOOL

Look first at some *practical matters* you may have overlooked or taken for granted.  For example, it is especially important to *check the calendar* of private schools.  Is this a year-round school?  Is this a September-to-June school?  Is this a multiple-track school which has no uniform beginning and end of the academic year? Is it a nine-week on, three-week off school, or instead a nine-month on, three-month off school?  If more than one of your children go there, will they be on different calendars?

Are school holidays consistent with your family's religious holidays?

Do you have to make special travel arrangements for your children, and will the school accommodate your circumstances?

Is the school independent of family involvement, or is substantial family involvement required?

Does the school have evening and weekend parent-teacher meetings for working parents, or are all such meetings held only during weekdays?

Does the school have special facilities for learning disabled, handicapped and other special children?

Does the school mainstream learning disabled and handicapped children with other children, and if so, is the experience positive for all the children?

Is the school for the elite, either academically or socially, or is the school a cross-sectional school?

Is the school racially balanced?

Is the school religiously balanced?

## RELIGIOUS SCHOOL QUESTIONS

*Look beyond the faith factor.* Some parochial schools move slowly; others progress quickly. Some are highly academic; others allow your child to move at his own pace.

What if the best match for your child is a religious school but not of the religion your family practices?

What if the school for your child is a religious school of your faith but is more (or less) religious than you are. Would your child be pressured? For example, you may be Jewish but not kosher, but the school is kosher. What will you have to do about lunches? Children embarrass easily when they do not do the same things as their peers.

What is the school's policy on non-participation in religious services? How much participation is required?

Will your child be the only student of a different faith attending the school or are there others (and how many)? For example, the enrollments at several prestigious Roman Catholic schools include a surprising proportion of non-Catholic students.

## DUAL CURRICULUM SCHOOLS

A dual curriculum school provides both secular and religious education, or courses both in English and another language. If your child attends such a program he is likely to have an extended school day.

For some children, the demands of the extended day are manageable, but others may become exhausted and/or regret the diminished time for after-school activities.

In addition, children with learning delays will not have enough opportunity or time for remediation. This can be a special disadvantage for your child when part of her day is taught in another language — for example, Hebrew.

## 7. PARENTAL INVOLVEMENT

Go through the school selection process recognizing what you want as a parent...and why. This is an important point. Some parents are most concerned that their child realize her full academic potential; others are more interested in finding a school to help their child navigate through life socially.

It will help to *recall your own schooling*. What was the experience like?...how did it help you develop?...what were the positives and negatives? There is likely to be a tremendous carryover from what you experienced that could color your objectivity about what you want now for your child. You may want him to have what you think you missed. Or you may take for granted aspects of your schooling that are no longer so readily available today.

## QUESTIONS ABOUT YOUR INVOLVEMENT

As you make your decision, you investigate what will be expected of you as an involved parent. Are you prepared to take on the commitment that will be demanded by the school you have chosen for your child?

**CASE STUDY:** Be aware of unwritten rules for parent involvement. One mother had to travel to another state for nine months to care for her dying mother and took her child with her. When they returned home, the school administrator told her that her child could not be reenrolled because of the mother's lack of continuing involvement in the school.

Are you willing to endure the driving and waiting around that will be necessary if you choose a school some distance from your home?  How about the extra driving to play dates, extracurricular activities, back-to-school nights, parent-teacher conferences...and much, much more?

Are you prepared for rejection if you apply to certain high-powered schools — for example, magnet schools?

Are you a staunch conservative and the school has a reputation for being progressive, if not downright liberal? Or do you wear Birkenstocks while the other parents wear Brooks Brothers?  In either case, will you and your child be comfortable with these differences?

Do parental activities seem likely to take on a country club aspect? Will you feel excluded from the school community if you are unable to participate in the round of lunches, picnics, fundraisers and school activities that occur during the day because you are a working parent?

Can you afford this investment of your personal, emotional and financial resources?  How will tuition increase — how frequently, by what increments — during the years your child is enrolled?  Are you likely to have to tighten your belt to make it through to her graduation?

## 8. PHYSICAL FACILITIES

An impressive physical facility does not guarantee a quality education, nor does a minimal physical facility threaten to provide a poor one. There is only the most *minimal correlation*, if any, between the appearance of a physical facility and the education that occurs there. (Exception: Air conditioning is essential in areas where extreme heat and humidity can make the classroom unbearable for several weeks or months each year.)

Still, the care with which the physical facility is treated and respected does give some indication of the school's philosophy. In addition, the availability of specific physical items — computer labs, well-equipped theaters, well-kept playing fields, comfortable and well-stocked libraries — indicate to what extent the school can deliver the promises it makes about its  curriculum.

The *balance between these various facilities* should ideally reflect your child's interests.  If the choice has to be made, is it more important that he participate in competition swimming in an Olympic-size pool or have access to the latest computer technology?  Make lists of the special facilities available at each school you are considering...give them a grade according to relative quality...then go over the lists with your child.

## TRADE-OFFS THAT MAY BE REQUIRED

**CASE STUDY:**  Jason feels that he isn't at a real school— there are no dances, no organized sports activities, no opportunities to socialize to the degree he wants to...and his social life is priority number one.  Should his parents agree that this is the wrong school for him or should they help him work harder to find other opportunities for socializing?

This can be a basic life lesson.  Sometimes you have to *give up some opportunities in order to get other things*.

In this case, Jason's parents have to recognize that it is not a problem that their son defines himself socially while they are focused on giving him a strong academic background —- not a problem, just a dilemma that needs attention and creative planning toward finding a solution.  They need to work with him to find social activities independent of the school.  In return, a happier Jason may discover that he can begin to relax and enjoy his school.

The worst-case scenario would be for Jason's parents to get stuck, as often happens, in seeing Jason's unhappiness as a terrible problem.  *When parents overreact, kids can get rebellious* instead of participating in finding ways of making both sides happy — and responding to Jason's two very real needs.

**CASE STUDY:**  One parent chose to transfer her son from his prep school back to public school because she  wanted her family to become an active part of their immediate community. The public school's activities were actually neighborhood activities, her son could walk to school with friends, the whole family felt relief that the commuting burden was eased, and a feeling of strong connection to other neighborhood families began to develop.

Because this family was very busy, this focus on their neighborhood gave them a sense of stability as a family unit that they could not get in other areas of their life.

In this case, the family's *need for a sense of community* was shared by the child involved, who was willing to trade off some of the academic advantages of prep school.

Most of us today don't have the kind of close, warm community connections we took for granted as children. In your search for the right school for your child, you may well want to think about the *kind of community* it has created for its students — and their parents — to share.

Both public and private schools are capable of addressing this issue in their own distinctive ways. Fostering a sense of shared community can build and affirm school pride. But be prepared to put your own shoulder to the wheel: if you are looking for a school that stresses community, it's only fair that you be *willing to contribute a substantial amount of parent time*. One admissions director told us frankly that her school specifically looks out for parents who are willing to give of themselves in any way they can. As she puts it, the "drop-off" parent who zips in and out of the school parking lot doesn't fit in well there.

On the other hand, if you feel that you have enough community in your life and just want a place to educate your child, there are *many schools that do not expect or want a great deal of parent participation*. Even in those situations, you still have to be involved, if only peripherally.

## IF YOU FEEL OVERWHELMED

Naturally, we like to feel that this book addresses the basic issues you will face as a parent trying to do what is best for your child when you evaluate schools...when you consider your child's individual personality...when you factor in your own needs...and when you deal with the likely consequences of your final decision.

Yet some situations can be extremely difficult and *might require expert counseling*. If you believe that you need such assistance in evaluating schools, evaluate your potential expert as well. Look for the following as a minimum:

1.  Credentials

2.  Experience

3.  Training

4.    Philosophy

5.    Specialties — for example: elementary schools, residential placement

## CHAPTER 5

# TOURING THE SCHOOL WITH YOUR EVALUATION FORMS

The best way to get to know a school is *to tour it*.

You'll get a sense of the actual day-to-day atmosphere that characterizes that particular school...see how the students feel and behave in class and outside...and learn how the teachers and students interact with each other.

More specifically, you can learn about programs and facilities that interest you, from sports to chemistry labs, and assess whether or not they will help your child.

At all times, you are asking yourself whether the school will be a good match for your child. Do you feel welcome? Is this a place you want to be? Does the classroom look inviting? Do the activities look interesting for someone at your child's level? Are the classrooms too noisy for your child? Or too deadly dull? Do the children seem sincerely eager and excited about being in school here? Does everyone dress neatly but not too formally? How do the play areas look? What about the food served at lunchtime?

By seeing the school for yourself, you will better understand what your child is likely to experience if he goes there.

## YOUR SCHOOL EVALUATION FORM

The *personal school evaluation forms* we have developed are included in this chapter. Think of these forms as your individual guide to seeing many different things in an organized, complete fashion.  They will also serve as a record of your tour, helping you to recall each school you visit and distinguish sharply between them.  As you fill in the blanks, a surprisingly clear picture will begin to emerge.

Our forms can be useful to you *if you are not changing schools*, because they are helpful tools for looking more closely at the school your child already attends. Even if you are satisfied with your child's educational experience, it is always a good idea to become more informed about her educational programs and processes.  Being informed is being powerful.

## WHY ARE THESE FORMS SO VALUABLE TO YOU?

Sometimes your judgment about a school can be misled by its overall appeal: the excitement of the winning debate team...the picturesque setting in a quiet valley...the well-scrubbed faces of the healthy kids.

Our evaluation forms should help you avoid that problem by helping you focus on the specific aspects of the school that will affect your child.  At the same time, it will build a total picture that can be matched with your whole child.  The admissions director who is so charming and forthcoming may be gone the next year, but the courses that make up the total curriculum will still be in place.

## USING YOUR EVALUATION FORMS

**Step One:**     Complete the *general information questions* before you go to the school.  As you can see, some of the questions can be answered by school officials, either in writing or over the telephone.  These questions provide basic background and should not really be considered a burden, even by overworked educators. The image of their school will be clarified, perhaps in ways they have not thought about before.

**Step Two:**     Take a *close look at the questions you will be filling out* during your tour.  Think a bit about how you will get the information you need.  (You may be seeking different kinds of information at different schools.) By preparing in this way, you can save time and also concentrate more fully on evaluating what you see.  In other words, you won't be so overwhelmed that you won't truly see what might be just right for your child.

HINT: *Put a checkmark* beside the items that are especially important for your child.

Step Three: When you tour the school, *listen well* so that you can absorb as much as possible. Aggressive questioning might be useful in other situations, but it could be misunderstood by the school. For example, too many questions about the curriculum could sound like hostility to the program—even though you just want to know more. Why should the director want to admit a child whose parents seem likely to raise arguments all year when other children have parents who are less intrusive?

If you do feel inclined to ask questions, focus on aspects of the tour. For example, how many children are in the classroom? What is the teacher-to-pupil ratio? (In other words, a class may have 20 students, but there could be more than one teacher.) Does the school make use of part-time teachers, aides, skills, teachers, community resource personnel?

HINT: As a basis of comparison, fill out the form for at least one other school.

## GENERAL GUIDELINES FOR YOUR EVALUATION

Even as you fill out the specific questions one by one, you will want to be attentive to several broad themes in our evaluation.

### 1. Physical Safety

Take note of the school's physical plant. How safe is it? Has the staff prepared well for emergencies? Is safety discussed frequently and clearly in the classroom? What about nearby traffic? You want to know that your child is in a safe place safely maintained.

### 2. Physical Attributes

A school might be located beside concrete, busy streets and have only the most limited esthetic attributes, but still offer a fine academic program. Another school might have green lawns dotted with stately trees, but not put enough emphasis on academics. The specifics of our evaluation form should help you see beneath the surface to the true story about each school you visit.

### 3. Class Size

Going from a large class to a small class can make all the difference for certain students, especially if they respond well to increased teacher attention and have difficulty expressing themselves in large-group situations.

In some cases, however, your child will be happiest in a situation where there is a larger number and greater variety of students.

Don't assume you know exactly what's best for your child, unless you have considered the issue before. Talk with her current teacher before making up your mind. It's not unusual for the child who is outspoken at home to wilt in the classroom, or vice versa.

### 4. Classroom Ambience

Look into the classrooms to see exactly what goes on in different grades under different teachers. Is the children's work displayed? (If you can do so without being disruptive, look at the level and type of work your child's future class would be doing.) Do the children look attentive and involved? Do they participate eagerly?

Do the teachers seem concerned, responsive, aware of what is happening around them? How do they handle disruptions, and do they ensure that students get the individual help they need? Does the classroom operate in a formal manner — for example, with assigned seats — or is it chaotic?

### 5. Curriculum

It is extremely important to look at the details of the school's curriculum and think about the potential benefits to your child.

Does the school follow the state guidelines? Do the types of courses available give your child enough flexibility? Do they provide the basics, offer review (if needed), or give him the opportunity to play to his academic strengths and work on his weaknesses?

Do not assume that you aren't qualified to ask questions about an algebra course, for example, because it's been so long since you were in school.  You don't need to know what is taught equation for equation: instead, you need to find out whether or not the course is appropriate for your child, based upon her gifts and needs and ambitions.  The school should be able to help you understand how any course they offer is, or is not, a good match for your child.

For your convenience there are two forms provided, one for elementary and one for secondary schools.

## SCHOOL EVALUATION — ELEMENTARY

Date _____

Student _____

Student's Current Grade _____     Birth Date _____

## GENERAL INFORMATION

School Name:_____

Address:_____

Phone ( ) _____     FAX ( ) _____

Grade Levels:     Elementary _____ to _____

Middle School _____ to _____

Secondary _____ to _____

Year School Established:_____

Type of School:

- ❑ coeducational
- ❑ males only
- ❑ females only
- ❑ non-denominational
- ❑ Board of Directors
- ❑ church/temple (denomination) _____
- ❑ parent-owned
- ❑ non-profit
- ❑ corporation
- ❑ other _____

Total Enrollment of School _____

Accept Exceptional Children?     ❑ yes     ❑ no

Types of special programs _____

Director/Principal _____

Director of Admissions _____

Accreditation _____

## FEES

Tuition:

New Family Fee _____

Entrance Fee _____

Scholarship/Reduced Fee Availability _____

_____

Application:

Fee _____        Date Due _____

Open Enrollment Period _____

## PHILOSOPHY OF EDUCATION AND GOALS

School's Philosophy of Education _____

_____

_____

_____

Goals of the School _____

_____

_____

_____

## CALENDAR AND SCHEDULE

School Calendar Year:     ❑ traditional     ❑ year round

    No. of minimum days _____     No. of pupil-free days _____

School Hours _____

    extended care hours _____

    staggered dismissal time? _____

Summer School _____

Vacation Schedule _____

Feeder Schools _____

After School Activities _____

## STAFF

Staff Personnel & Days Available:

    teachers _____

_____

_____

    psychologist _____

    nurse _____

    speech _____

    librarian _____

    resource specialist _____

    special education classes _____

    other _____

Who is trained in CPR? _____

Teaching Staff:

    training & credentials _____

    teacher in-service/continuing education requirements _____

    _____

    male/female ratio _____


Counseling Services (Guidance & Mental Health Services):

    psychological assessment _____

    psychological counseling _____


Aides:

    ❏    in classroom

        days & hours _____

        what training required _____


## ENROLLMENT PROCEDURES AND INFORMATION


Entrance & Placement Criteria

    sibling priority _____

    initial interview _____

    informal assessment _____

    formal assessment _____

    academic standards _____

    social/emotional development standards _____

    retention and promotion policy _____


Need for Advance Enrollment Reservation _____

Mid-year enrollment _____

Contract _____

Open Enrollment Period _____

Waiting List Procedures _____

Continuing Students Automatically Progress to Middle School? _____

Need to Reapply for Middle School by (date) _____


## TRANSPORTATION

    place for bicycle _____

    carpool arrangements _____

    bus:    school _____

            public _____


## CLASSROOMS

Classes:

    anticipated openings _____

    class size _____

    student/teacher ratio _____

    age/grade groupings in each class _____

    racially balanced _____

    student/aide ratio _____

Classroom Ambiance:

    student work displayed _____

    classroom organization _____

    atmosphere _____

    cleanliness _____

    visually stimulating _____

    size of room _____

bulletin boards _____

storage space for each student _____

size of room (large enough for # of students)? _____

## CURRICULUM

Homework:

how presented?

- ❑ orally
- ❑ on chalk board
- ❑ written on paper
- ❑ in assignment book or voice mail
- ❑ posted on bulletin board
- ❑ daily, weekly, long-term

grade in which homework is commenced _____

Assessment Criteria:

- ❑ formal assessment of student
- ❑ gifted assessment
- ❑ special education assessment
- ❑ refer to other professionals for assessment

Curriculum/Instruction:

provision for individual needs _____

provision for individualized instruction _____

grouping _____

reading/language arts approach & materials _____

math program _____

% teacher-directed lessons _____

% aide directed lessons _____

% independent study _____

degree of student participation _____

physical education _____

team teaching _____

cross-age tutoring/peer teaching _____

Supplemental Programs:

foreign language(s) _____

science _____

horticulture _____

animals _____

shop classes _____

home economics classes _____

art/music/theater arts/dance _____

library _____

keyboarding _____

computer instruction _____

computer lab _____

computers in classrooms _____

athletic programs _____

    ❏ competitive   ❏ non-competitive

field trips _____

travel programs _____

remedial tutoring _____

cross age tutoring/peer group teaching _____

community service programs _____

library _____

    hours/days _____

Special Education:

   programs for visually impaired _____

   programs for deaf & hard of hearing _____

   mainstream opportunities _____

   adapted physical education _____

   sensory-integration training _____

   perceptual-motor training _____

   speech and language _____

   resource specialist program (RSP) _____

   individualized education plans _____

## RELIGIOUS SCHOOLS

   dual curriculum _____

   classes in religion _____

   religious services:    ❏ optional    ❏ mandatory

## PHYSICAL PLANT

Play Areas & Equipment:

   Playing Surface:

        ❏  dirt          ❏  wood chips

        ❏  grass         ❏  shredded bark

        ❏  sand          ❏  concrete

        ❏  asphalt

   Equipment Safety:

      maintained well _____

      how close together _____

      height off ground _____

Supervision:

  training/license _____

  coaches _____

  use of supplemental park sites _____

Physical Plant:

  cleanliness _____

  custodial service _____

  auditorium _____

Cafeteria:

  ❑  cold lunch            ❑  hot lunch

  ❑  health-conscious      ❑  junk food

  prices_____

Security Provisions:

  personnel _____

  procedures for picking up a child _____

  _____

  locked physical plant _____

Is this a non-smoking campus? _____

Or are there designated smoking areas? _____

## PARENT PARTICIPATION

Visitation by Parents:

  any time _____        arranged _____        check in with office _____

Parent Teacher Association(PTA) _____

What is requested or expected of parent participation:

    classroom _____       field trips _____

    fund raising _____       resource room _____

    supervision of activities, sports _____

Fund Raising Activities:

    what _____

    who does it (parent,child) _____

    how many per year _____

Organization of School Projects/Activities _____

_____

School Advisory Council _____

Parent Conferences:

    frequency _____       flexibility _____

    arrangement of additional conferences _____

Parent Education Seminars _____

## BEHAVIOR MANAGEMENT/DISCIPLINE

Behavior Management/Problem Solving Techniques:

    % done by teacher _____

    % done by students _____

    problem solving dialogues _____

making restitution _____

referral to director _____

isolation _____

corporal punishment _____

time out _____

evidence of respect and courtesy _____


School standards for respect, courtesy, manners and safety _____

_____

_____

_____

_____


## OVERALL IMPRESSIONS


Overall impressions about the school _____

_____

_____

_____

_____

_____

_____


Person completing this form _____

Date _____

# SCHOOL EVALUATION — SECONDARY

Date _____

Student _____

Student's Current Grade _____     Birth Date _____

## GENERAL INFORMATION

School Name:_____

Address:_____

Phone (    ) _____     FAX  (    ) _____

Grade Levels:       Elementary _____ to _____

                    Middle School _____ to _____

                    Secondary _____ to _____

Year School Established:_____

Type of School:

- ❏ coeducational
- ❏ males only
- ❏ females only
- ❏ non-denominational
- ❏ Board of Directors
- ❏ church/temple (denominational) _____
- ❏ parent-owned
- ❏ non-profit
- ❏ corporation
- ❏ other _____

Total Enrollment of School _____

Accept Exceptional Children?    ❑ yes    ❑ no

    areas _____

Director/Principal _____

Director of Admissions _____

Accreditation _____

## FEES

Tuition:

New Family Fee _____

Entrance Fee _____

Scholarship/Reduced Fee Availability _____

_____

Application:

Fee _____     Date Due _____

Open Enrollment Period _____

## PHILOSOPHY OF EDUCATION AND GOALS

School's Philosophy of Education _____

_____

_____

Goals of the School _____

_____

_____

## CALENDAR AND SCHEDULE

School Calendar Year:    ❏ traditional    ❏ year round

    No. of minimum days _____

    No. of pupil-free days _____

School Hours: _____

Staggered Dismissal Time? _____

Summer School _____

Vacation Schedule _____

Feeder Schools _____


After School Activities: _____

    school sponsored _____

    extra curricular _____

    social activities _____

## STAFF

Staff Personnel and Days Available:

    teachers _____

    _____

    _____

    psychologist _____

    nurse _____

    speech _____

    librarian _____

    resource specialist _____

    special education classes _____

    other _____

Who is trained in CPR? _____

Teaching Staff:

    training & credentials _____

    teacher in-service/continuing education requirements _____

    _____

    male/female ratio _____

Counseling Services (Guidance & Mental Health Services):

    psychological assessment _____

    psychological counseling _____

    vocational/career counseling _____

Aides:

    in classroom _____    days & hours _____

    what training required _____

## ENROLLMENT PROCEDURES AND INFORMATION

Entrance & Placement Criteria:

    ❑ sibling priority      ❑ initial interview

    ❑ informal assessment    ❑ formal assessment

    academic standards _____

    social/emotional development standards _____

    _____

    retention/promotion policy _____

    _____

Need for Advance Enrollment Reservation _____

Mid-year enrollment _____

Contract _____

Open Enrollment Period _____

Waiting List Procedures _____

_____

Continuing Students Automatically Progress to Upper School? _____

Need to Reapply for Upper School by (date) _____

## TRANSPORTATION

    place for bicycle _____

    carpool arrangements _____

    cars:

        parking for students _____

        protected parking _____

        priority parking for carpools _____

        priority parking for females _____

        escort to car for females (after dark) _____

    bus:

        school _____

        public _____

## CLASSROOMS

Classes:

    anticipated openings _____

    class size _____    student/teacher ratio _____

    age/grade groupings in each class _____

    racially balanced _____

    student/aide ratio _____

Classroom Ambiance:

 student work displayed _____

 classroom organization _____

 atmosphere _____

 cleanliness _____

 visually stimulating _____

 size of room _____

 bulletin boards _____

 storage space for each student _____

 size of room (large enough for # of students?) _____

## CURRICULA

Homework:

 how presented?

 ❏ orally    ❏ on chalk board

 ❏ written on paper    ❏ in assignment book

 ❏ posted on bulletin board    ❏ voice mail

 ❏ daily    ❏ weekly    ❏ long-term

 distribution of projects:

 ❏ daily    ❏ weekly    ❏ long-term

Assessment Criteria:

 ❏    formal assessment of student is done

 ❏    gifted assessment

 ❏    special education assessment

 ❏    refer to other professionals for assessment?

Curriculum/Instruction:

provision for individual needs _____

provision for individualized instruction _____

grouping _____

reading/language arts approach & materials _____

math program _____

% teacher-directed lessons _____

% aide directed lessons _____

% independent study _____

degree of student participation _____

physical education _____

team teaching _____

cross-age tutoring/peer teaching _____


Supplemental Programs:

foreign language(s) _____

science _____

horticulture _____

animals _____

shop classes _____

home economics classes _____

art/music/theater arts/dance _____

library _____

keyboarding _____

computer instruction _____

computer lab _____        hours _____

computers in classrooms _____

athletic programs _____

❑ competitive     ❑ non-competitive

field trips _____

travel programs _____

remedial tutoring _____

cross age tutoring/peer group teaching _____

community service programs _____

community internship programs _____

drivers education _____

library _____

    hours/days _____

    computerized service available _____

    shared resources with other schools and/or universities

    (Ex.: book transfer) _____

community internship program _____

community volunteer work available _____


Special Education:

    programs for visually impaired _____

    programs for deaf & hard of hearing _____

    mainstream opportunities _____

    adapted physical education _____

    sensory-integration training _____

    perceptual-motor training _____

    speech and language _____

    resource specialist program (RSP) _____

    individualized education plans _____

    other _____


Religious Schools:

    dual curriculum _____

classes in religion _____

religious services:     ❑ optional     ❑ mandatory

## PHYSICAL PLANT

Play Areas & Equipment:

    playing surface:

        ❑ dirt           ❑ wood chips

        ❑ grass         ❑ shredded bark

        ❑ sand          ❑ concrete

        ❑ asphalt

Equipment Safety:

    maintained well _____

    how close together _____

    height off ground _____

Supervision:

    training/license _____

    coaches _____

    use of supplemental park sites _____

Physical Plant:

    cleanliness _____

    custodial service _____

    auditorium _____

Cafeteria:

    ❑ cold lunch       ❑ hot lunch

❏ health conscious          ❏ junk food

prices _____

Food Trucks:

❏ health food          ❏ junk food

Security Provisions:

personnel _____

procedures for picking up a child _____

_____

locked physical plant _____

Is this a non-smoking campus? _____

Or are there designated smoking areas? _____

## OTHER

school store _____

school credit card _____

lunch & snack cards _____

cash allowed on campus _____

## PARENT PARTICIPATION

Visitation by Parents _____

Parent Teacher Association (PTA) _____

What is requested or expected of parent participation:

classroom _____          field trips _____

fund raising _____          resource room _____

supervision of activities, sports _____

organization of school projects/activities _____

_____


Fund Raising Activities:

   what _____

   who does it (parent,child) _____

   how many per year _____


School Advisory Council _____


Parent Conferences:

   frequency _____          flexibility _____

   arrangement of additional conferences _____


Parent Education Seminars _____


## BEHAVIOR MANAGEMENT/DISCIPLINE


Behavior Management/Problem Solving Techniques:

   % done by teacher _____

   % done by students _____

   problem solving dialogues _____

   making restitution _____

   referral to director _____

   isolation _____

   corporal punishment _____

   time out _____

evidence of respect & courtesy _____

School standards for respect, courtesy, manners and safety: _____
_____

## OVERALL IMPRESSIONS

Overall impressions about the school _____
_____
_____
_____
_____
_____
_____

Person completing this form _____

Date _____

**CHAPTER 6**

# PREPARING YOUR CHILD'S APPLICATION

The application process is so central to the course of choosing your child's school that you might want to consider blocking out a significant amount of time for dealing with applications in an organized way.

We strongly recommend that both parents work together, when possible. It's best to make a rough draft before actually filling in the application. This background work will give you a chance to look closely at your child and yourself as you decide what is most important to get across to the school.

Keep a file on each school you apply to and include a photocopy of your completed application with the date you mailed it in. Confirm that it did indeed reach the school. If possible, it would be better to deliver the application in person. This not only assures that it is not lost in the mail but also gives you an opportunity to tell the school again about your strong interest.

Here's some advice on how you can take charge of the application process:

1.  Start collecting application forms and related materials at least a year before your child would be entering the schools you've put on your list. Postponement can be fatal.

    Telephone each of these schools to find out what each specifically requires in terms of paperwork, fees, and independent evaluations.

    Are applications *made available on a certain date*?

If so and the school is very popular, your "competition" may be out in force hours beforehand. We know of one case where anxious parents began lining up at 5 a.m. for applications to be distributed at 8 a.m. This is a rare situation, of course, but it is always best to request the necessary forms early.

2.  Note the **cutoff date** for filing the applications. They can vary widely, even within a single community. Some schools can be as strict about the postmark, by the way, as the IRS. Don't lose your opportunity because of a technicality.

3.  Complete and return the application form **as soon as possible**! Some schools expect your applications to be completed as early as September or October, a year before your child can enroll.

4.  For a helpful dose of reality, find out as much as you can about the **profile of the class** to be chosen. For example, how many places are available to girls, how many to boys? How many spots are likely to be taken by siblings of current or past students, by children of graduates or staff, by selected minority groups, and so on.

The school should be forthcoming about these statistics, which certainly affect your child's chances for admission.

**POSITIVE ATTITUDE HINT:** Don't let yourself feel that a school is being unreasonably rigid about cutoff dates and other application procedures, such as the scheduling of interviews. Try to understand that a hasty, last-minute application not only inconveniences school officials, who are often overworked, but also suggests that you and your child aren't really all that interested in their school or don't value their time. Also, the reality today is that some private schools have so many applicants that it becomes impossible to schedule last-minute interviews.

## PLAN OUT THE APPLICATION PROCESS CAREFULLY

Once you have the application in hand, make a list of the *additional information* or *supplementary materials* you are required to assemble:

❑ Medical reports

❑ Teacher recommendations

❑ Personal recommendations

❑ Testing information

❑ Grade transcripts

❑ Professional evaluations

❑ Recent photos

Begin assembling this basic information *immediately*, because most of these items will require the cooperation of someone else and unforeseen obstacles can intervene:

A professional may be too busy to schedule a medical or educational evaluation without plenty of advance notice....

The teacher who would write the warmest recommendation for your child may transfer elsewhere, if you don't ask right away....

Office assistants who know how to put their hands on transcripts or medical reports can be away on vacation or personal business if you wait until the last minute...

Finally, you do not want to put friends, neighbors, coaches and others under unfair pressure to write a personal recommendation overnight.

As a purely practical matter, everyone will be better able to give you the best possible information or reference if you *give them enough time* to come through for you and your child.

**POSITIVE ATTITUDE HINT:** If you're the kind of person who likes to take control of things, let that character trait work for you during the application process.

On the other hand, you can organize, plan and produce only up to a point...

Then, like it or not, the matter is out of your hands. You can't control whether your child's application goes to the top or the bottom of the heap. Accept that. Some people react to this fact of life by pressuring school officials or erupting at home. Calm down. In the final analysis, all you can do is present the strongest, most honest, most personalized case for your child. The institution will make the decision.

## TRUE TALES OF PARENTS GOING OVER THE EDGE

We don't make these stories up...

One father we knew became so overwrought during the application process that he went to a certain school on the morning applications were first made available, even though his son was not applying there. He didn't have the academic background necessary. By finding out who was standing in line and comparing the list with those who were accepted later, this father was able to say to his friends, "See? Lindsay tried, and she didn't get in either. Gavin was rejected, too."

And at an Open House at another prestigious institution, an eagle-eyed mother stood in the parking lot with her daughter as other parents picked up applications. "Martha doesn't stand a chance," she was overheard saying. "Don't worry. There are only so many spots for girls, and she's no competition for you."

## WHAT WILL MAKE YOUR CHILD'S RECOMMENDATION STAND OUT?

The schools you choose may ask for personal recommendations from a variety of sources: present and former school teachers, school administrators, dance or voice teachers outside school, scout leaders, ministers or rabbis, and so forth.

Just as important as choosing the right people to write recommendations, however, is taking time to understand the *intent* behind a particular school's request for recommendations:

Should a former school teacher write about your child's academic gifts or evidence of strong character? Or both?

Does the soccer coach need to stress your child's competitive instincts on the field, or her reliability at practice, or her leadership qualities?
For the most effective possible recommendations, you must:

1. Find out exactly what kind of information or evaluation your school wants from your references, then

2. Explain clearly to your references what is required.

You are NOT telling them what to say, of course, but you MUST make as clear as possible what areas the school really wants to know about: intelligence or character or comparative level of maturity, social skills or artistic talent or eagerness to learn, sense of humor or knack for lab work....Whatever!

Your references will appreciate knowing how to make their recommendations useful, and their letters will definitely stand out from the crowd if they are focused and specific.

## RECOMMENDATIONS: BLEND AND MIX WELL

In addition to whatever specific areas the school wants your references to address, you should select at least one person who can write about your whole family and your *contributions to the community*:

For example, if you or your spouse helped out with your daughter's swim team, ask the coach to write a letter about her that includes your participation.

Make certain such references are specific: "When we needed to raise money for the band trip, Jim and his mother made cookies for the bake sale, his dad totaled up the receipts, and his sister brought her friends over from another school to buy stuff."

What your school learns from such examples is that you and your family are likely to pitch in when needed. Parental involvement is a priceless asset to any school, no matter how wealthy or prestigious it is.

Also, such specific incidents will brighten up your school interview [see Chapter 7]. For example, the interviewer can begin, "Well, I see you and your mom are both serious about competitive swimming." This personal touch breaks the ice and helps your child present herself as an individual.

## HOW DO YOU DESCRIBE YOURSELF AND YOUR CHILD?

For many of you, the most daunting part of the application process will be writing about yourself or your child when such parental statements are required.

Make this an opportunity, not a burden. If you are asked to supply *biographical information about yourself*, you can help your child by explaining to the school what kind of parent you've tried to be...what goals you and your spouse set for yourself in the family...what kind of relationship you have with your child and how it has grown over the years.

When two parents are involved in the application process, *work together* on the parental statement, both in writing about your parental goals and in describing your child. [An extra benefit: when you go to the parental interview, you will already have clarified on paper what you both think and can present a cohesive picture of your child and your family.]

*Think before you write*: the temptation is to plunge in without thinking about what you really feel from your unique point of view as the parent of this particular child. This application is not meant to be a cold, precise academic exercise. You are writing as a loving parent. Certainly, this is the right time to put into words the enjoyment you feel in being the parent of your child.

*Don't neglect the obvious*: be neat, and write clearly...just as your second grade teacher taught you.

For best results, don't consider your parental statement to be a casual letter or free-form statement. Write out a rough draft. While you let it sit for a couple of days, jot down any new ideas that come to you — anecdotes that make a good point about your child's character, quotes from him or his friends or teachers, feelings you had when he was younger, more direct ways of saying what you mean. When you reread your first draft, change or delete anything that seems overstated, vague, unfelt, irrelevant or insincere. Have a friend or teacher read your final draft, if that seems a helpful idea.

*Be honest*: Try not to exaggerate your child's strengths or dismiss too airily any problems or weaknesses.

1.  DO NOT over glamorize your child.

2.  DO present a picture that approaches reality as nearly as possible, school officials will instantly spot a con job.  Don't forget: they see these kids every day.

Facing the truth about a problem is not inconsistent with optimism.  For example, you can point out that your son has progressed from being extremely shy to taking the initiative in certain social situations.  If he still seems somewhat timorous in new surroundings (e.g., the school interview), explain that at least the trend seems to be toward greater confidence in himself.

By the same token, you may want to anticipate the school's reaction by showing that you recognize that your child's strengths are not without drawbacks.  You can explain that you are pleased by your daughter's competitiveness, for example, because it reveals a drive to succeed.  You might also want to point out that you feel sometimes that she needs to learn to recognize the line between striving to win and aggression.

By giving a *reasonably balanced picture*, you do not present an artificial (and unhelpful) view of your child.

*Give concrete examples*: the minute you begin writing or talking in abstract terms about your child, you've lost it.  You just aren't saying anything. Rather than note vaguely that your son is musically gifted, explain that he plays Bartok on the violin but can't stand Haydn, or hates grunge but writes his own alternative rock lyrics. After all, this is the fun part of filling out the application: the chance to tell stories about your own child.

If *specific talents* help portray your child's personality, *specific passions* may tell even more of the story.

**CASE STUDIES:**  One parent thought it a bit strange when we urged her to tell the school about her daughter's passion for collecting rocks. "Wherever we go on a family trip," she wrote in her parental statement, "Lisa somehow finds rocks that fit into the categories that interest her; you should see her room: wall-to-wall rocks!" In this way, the admissions council learned a tremendous amount about the girl's organizational skills, inventiveness, lively curiosity and determination.

Instead of describing his son as "having incredible visual skills" or some such abstract characteristic, one father explained on an application that his young son had learned on his own to read architectural plans during a renovation of their house and had begun looking in their friends' houses for examples of "balloon construction", a term he had picked up from the drawings.

Or, instead of merely describing her daughter as "family-oriented," one mother wrote that the girl organized marionette shows in the den for her younger siblings and their playmates, including playlets that taught them safety lessons in an amusing way.

*Use quotes whenever possible*: if a teacher wrote a particularly interesting comment on a report card or paper, use it! Any quotes from educational professionals are invaluable. They are like reviewers' blurbs, helping a stranger get a useful insight into the uniqueness of your child.

A driver in the car pool, a cafeteria worker, a parent of a playmate, even a relative — anyone outside the immediate family is a potential source for quotes. Not only do they bring different points of view; they also see aspects of your child that may not be obvious in the home.

## SHOULD YOU TELL THE TRUTH ABOUT THERAPY?

Generally speaking, an application might ask something like, "Have you had psychological services?" In our experience, the school is interested in learning about significant psychological problems, NOT necessarily about therapeutic sessions to provide guidance to better parenting or to improve communication between family members.

Nonetheless, if you and/or your family has seen someone for advice, you should briefly and clearly explain the circumstances and the results. Some schools will consider your experience with this kind of psychological assistance to be an advantage. Others may not.

Whatever your family treatment history, however, you should tell the truth.

## HOW DO YOU GET THE MOST EFFECTIVE LETTERS FROM OTHERS?

Suppose your child is likely to get fairly weak referrals from his teachers....

Worse, suppose only one teacher will give her a strong letter...

And what if a sixth-grade teacher, say, has been continually abusing his power to recommend students to middle school by saying to you, "I guess I will have to tell them about Clara's impudence to me, unless there is a change in her behavior....."

What if you know that the school counselor, for whatever reason, openly dislikes your child?

All of the above — and similar unfortunate situations — can happen in the real world, since teachers are human beings who can have biases or feel slights or have beliefs about child-rearing which are different from yours. You may sometimes have to face the fact that you will have to work extra hard to get good recommendations.

***Seek a balance***: if one teacher is likely to give a weak or negative appraisal of your child, make sure that two others will produce positive referrals.

**CASE STUDY:** Josh felt wonderful about his sixth-grade year. Devoted to writing poetry and bird watching, he tends to lose himself in daydreams. The year before, his fifth-grade teacher delighted in his poetic style of writing and his poetic style of being. She thought he was a joy to teach.

But these very qualities drove his sixth-grade teacher to distraction. She began picking on him frequently, or so it seemed to Josh. She made clear that he was far from being her favorite student. Even as Josh blithely enjoyed her class, his parents grew more and more nervous about having to ask for her recommendation to middle school, as required.

We suggested that they ask the school for a second recommendation form (or a photocopy) to give to the fifth-grade teacher. In this case, there was no problem. Should a school refuse to provide the form, you can always ask the other teacher to write a letter of recommendation and send it directly to the admissions office.

## WHAT ABOUT THE WEAK OR NEGATIVE REFERRAL?

In some cases, you might want to ask a teacher to return the referral form directly to you. Explain that you understand that she or he might not feel comfortable giving a strongly positive referral; you want to know what you are dealing with. (This is a fair request, by any standards.)

If the referral is as weak as you fear, attach a note along with your application that explains calmly and clearly your view of the situation. For example, you might write, "Ms. Colleti is a dedicated teacher whose conventional ideas about discipline came into conflict with our son's previous experiences in more loosely structured classrooms. We feel that her view of Josh may be colored by this conflict."

## WHAT ABOUT THE DIRECTOR WHO DOESN'T LIKE MY CHILD?

In this case, you are not a moving target....You are a sitting duck.

The director's report will be mailed directly to the school. In other words, she can hit you with her eyes closed.

You can bring up the problem during the school interview, if you expect it to be serious...or you can refer to it *briefly* in your parental statement. That puts the ball in the school's court, if they want to pursue the matter.

## WHAT ABOUT POTENTIAL CONFLICTS AT THE PRESENT SCHOOL?

If you are considering a transfer from your child's present school, it is wise to be wary. Quite possibly, one or more teachers or officials will resent your decision and (consciously or not) create obstacles. Besides, you may regret rocking the boat if your child's transfer application is denied.

Discuss the potential problem with admissions officials at the schools you are considering. Many are sensitive to the issue and will suggest that you wait to ask for teacher referrals and grade transcripts until late in the application process — perhaps even after the school interview and submission of the rest of your child's application materials.

At that time, bring all of your skills as a public relations rep for your child into play. Present the application as diplomatically as possible. You must do your best to let everyone save face all around, even if your child is moving from a little-known private school to the ultimate chi-chi prep school. Explain that the new school is likely to be a better match for your child, or more convenient, or more attractive because of the friends he has made there. Whatever the reason you give, it must not imply any criticism of the current school.

Even so, it is a good idea to get back-up evaluations from your child's favorite teachers, just in case some official's prejudice against the transfer produces a negative evaluation.

On the other hand, the response at your child's current school may go completely in the opposite direction. Experienced, concerned staff should recognize that your decision to transfer is a matter of moving your child on to the next step, not necessarily an act of criticism. They may become more responsive to his needs. They may feel relief, in some situations, that he is transferring to a school situation that is more appropriate for him. Their pride in their work may help them focus on preparing him as fully as possible for the coming change.

**CASE STUDY:** The parents of third-grader Marcy came to us for an evaluation. "We think we have a very gifted child," the father explained, "but the school complains that she is inattentive and disrupts the class by acting out." An older sister in the same school had never had any problems there, so they were unprepared for this reaction.

Our evaluation of Marcy showed that she was indeed highly gifted and likely to be bored with the school's conventional curriculum.

The school staff tried to respond by giving her more challenging work, but Marcy was still bored. When her parents decided to enroll her elsewhere, the staff was understanding and supportive.

In fact, this was a situation with a completely satisfying result, because everyone understood the true nature of the problem and was interested in Marcy's welfare. No one's ego got in the way. At her new school, Marcy flourished, and her behavior problems disappeared.

## PHOTOS

Even when the application notes that a photograph of your child is "optional," it is helpful to send one along. Quite simply, the picture helps school officials identify and recall her, a distinct advantage throughout the admission and placement process.

*But read the instructions*: if the school asks for your child's portrait, don't send a shot of the whole family…and vice versa.  Whatever their reasons, give them what they want.

*And don't go Hollywood*: the best photo is the most revealing, which is likely to be a candid shot or a conventional school picture.  Not only is an expensive formal studio portrait likely to be unhelpful; it might also suggest that you have gone to the time, expense and trouble to have a picture made especially for the application…not exactly the best ordering of priorities.

Remember: You want to be seen as cooperative, not desperate.

**SUMMING UP:**  For quick and easy review, the following list breaks down and amplifies the information in this chapter.

## A CHECKLIST OF APPLICATION DO'S AND DON'TS

When you are trying to describe your child from your own perspective as a parent…

### *DO give very specific examples.*
- For example, "We've always noticed that Amy has a very enquiring mind. She took apart many things and always put them back together in a new way." This adds concrete detail.

- Or, "Jamie always loved a story, whether we read to him or he listened to a tape.  Whether it's about his grandmother in Maine or Babar the Elephant, he is fascinated."

- And put yourself in the description.  For example,  "I like the way Eloise speaks up for herself and is never afraid to ask questions."

- Or, "It astonishes me sometimes that Greg tries always to see the other person's side of a situation."

### *DON'T be vague or depend upon cliches.*
- For example, the eyes glaze over at "My child is a source of constant joy and comfort to me."

- And, no information about a unique individual is conveyed by "My darling child would be an asset to your school."

- Nor is curiosity aroused by the general statement, "He has such charm and personality that everyone mentions it."

When you assemble the letters of referral and recommendation...

### DO choose carefully which letters to send.

- Some choices are obviously politically helpful. If you're lucky enough to have a friend who is on the school's board, she's top of the pile. Also, a letter from a family actively involved and/or well regarded by the faculty and staff is a good choice.

- To provide a reliable overview, ask your pediatrician or anyone else who has had ongoing contact with your child. (In the case of an application to kindergarten, you will have to have a letter from the director of any preschool program your child attended.) Definitely include a letter from at least one of your child's current teachers and also from one other person outside the school.

- The most valuable letters are the most specific and concrete ones: for example, the soccer coach should explain exactly how your daughter contributes to the team's success, not just comment that he's "so happy to have her on the team."

### DON'T stack the deck.

- Too many letters will probably bring you diminishing returns.

- If you *do* add letters to the basic four or five, make sure that they are strongly positive and provide a unique perspective. For example, you certainly should include a recommendation like the following from a piano teacher: "In the 20 years I've been teaching music, Philip is one of the few children I've seen with an immediate sense of rhythm and patterning of music, and I have watched him go from playing the notes to learning to compose in his own voice."

## WHAT ABOUT FINANCIAL AID?

Your application for financial aid will be handled separately, perhaps by a financial aid officer or special committee.

Ideally, of course, the admissions staff are not told who has need of financial assistance.

## SAMPLE APPLICATION FORM

(This composite sample application form will give you an example of commonly asked questions.)

Applicant's Name

Nickname (if any)

Date of Birth                               Male/Female

Birthplace

Applying for Grade _____
Application for Grade _____
Grade Entering _____

Grade to Be Completed _____        Date _____

Date of Previous Application

Previous School/Type of School
School Last Attended/Type of School

Siblings Attending This School/Names/Ages
Siblings Who Have Attended This School

Relatives Attending This School
Relatives Who Have Attended This School

Students You Know Attending This School
Students You Know Who Have Attended This School

Legacy

Current School/Type of School/Address/Telephone/Head of School/Current Teacher

Applicant's Address/Telephone

Siblings: Name/Age/Present School

Mother's Name
    Legal Name of Mother/Guardian

Father's Name
    Legal Name of Father/Guardian

Mother's Occupation and Title/Business
    Name/Address/Telephone

Father's Occupation and Title/Business
    Name/Address/Telephone

Religious Affiliation

Degrees and Institutions Obtained at for Mother and for Father

Marital Status of Parents: Together ____    Separated ____    Divorced ____

Mother Deceased

Father Deceased

If parents are divorced:
    Child resides with/student lives with
    Correspondence sent to
    Financial responsibility rests with/Tuition to be paid by

Mother Remarried

Father Remarried

Custody

Visitation Rights

Step-Mother: Occupation & Title/Business
    Name/Address/Telephone

Step-Father: Occupation & Title/Business
    Name/Address/Telephone

Please list any community, civic, or charitable organizations of which you are a member

Please list the type of activities/vacations your family participates in as a family

Please name two or three parenting books that have influenced your child-rearing practices

Names of Child's Maternal Grandparents/Address/Telephone

Names of Child's Paternal Grandparents/Address/Telephone

Emergency Name/Person to Contact in an Emergency/Telephone Numbers

Family Doctor/Address/Telephone

Student Health:

    Has the applicant ever had a serious illness? If so, please specify and tell for how long

    Has the applicant ever had a serious operation?  If so, please specify

    Are there any medical, physical or psychological problems of which the school should be aware?

    Has the applicant ever had psychological counseling?  If yes, please explain

Has the applicant ever needed professional help with reading or learning problems?  If yes, please explain

Has the applicant ever had professional tutoring?  If so, please specify type and for what length of time

Has the applicant ever studied a foreign language?  If so, please specify

Academic Interests

Achievements/Any Offices Held/Any Awards

Athletic Interests

Special Talents

Extra-curricular Activities

Hobbies

Social Involvement Activities

Note here any tests the candidate/applicant has taken for educational learning disabilities

Parents' Comments/Please describe your child's personality from a parental perspective to help the Admissions Officer get to know him/her better

## CHAPTER 7

# THE INTERVIEW

The interview is a *crucial step* in the application process:

1.  Scheduled after you have submitted your child's application to the admissions committee, the interview is the best way for the admissions officer to get to know your child and your family.

2.  Also, the interview is an excellent opportunity for you to learn more about the school. This is the time to ask questions, to find out whether or not this school is the best educational choice for your child.

Keep these two goals constantly in mind — presenting yourself and your child to the school, finding out as much as you can about the school — as you plan for the all-important interview.

The impression you and your child present in person is likely to mean more in the long run than much of the information on the written application. Prepare by reading and thinking carefully about this chapter.

*There are many different types of interviews.* Usually, an elementary school will interview parents and their child separately. The child may perhaps be evaluated along with a group of other children rather than individually.

As your child gets older, it is more likely that you will be interviewed together, or even as an entire family, but time constraints might require the school to interview an older child in a group situation, too. This is another reason to send in your application early. In a group interview, one person might dominate, answering all of the questions. Your child, especially if somewhat shy and withdrawn, would be at a disadvantage.

**POSITIVE ATTITUDE HINTS:** *Don't assume you're guaranteed a spot.* You may have successfully performed major surgery on the headmaster's sister, but passing along that information to the admissions interviewer may not help your child's case at all. In the interview, you are selling yourself as a parent, not as a professional.

*You may pay the tuition bills, but the interviewer is not your employee.* Don't breeze into the office and whip out your Filofax. Don't bring along your beeper. When one of our clients took his cellular phone to an interview and took calls, he was inadvertently giving out a message loud and clear:   "I'm more important than you; your questions don't require my full attention." He was showing disrespect for the interviewer, for the school and for his child's best interests.

*This is a professional situation.* Another of our clients took along her teething four month old to an interview for her five year old daughter. Soon, the baby's cries were drowning out the interviewer's questions. The interview had to be curtailed.

*Your child's emotional well-being is top priority.* No matter how young she is, your child will sense any anxiety you have about the interview...and then internalize those fears. The result? Everyone's stress level zooms...your child becomes more anxious and unhappy...your interview bombs.

*Set a positive tone.* Go easy on your child. Go easy on yourself. Set the stage by helping your child see that the interview can be fun, a time to talk about his favorite games and best friends...a time to tell stories...a time to learn about the activities at the school. During the interview, be open. Don't resist the process or show hostility. The school has enough problems without bringing another disagreeable parent on board.

*Concentrate.* If you know that the interview might be interrupted by a potential emergency at home or the office, notify the interviewer at the beginning of the meeting. Usually, this is preferable to rescheduling, especially if the appointment has been difficult to arrange. Apologize for the anticipated interruption. If at all possible, avoid this kind of situation.

*Let the interviewer take the lead*. But if you begin feeling anxious, say so. Trying to pretend otherwise may come across as aloofness. Let yourself be excited and eager. Take a few calming breaths, and try your best to relax.

## HOW SHOULD DIVORCED PARENTS PREPARE?

If possible, both parents should go to the school interview. In many families today, however, joint custody arrangements and other consequences of divorce produce a number of people who share legal, financial and emotional responsibility for a child.

Because it is unwieldy, not to say unfair, to expect an interviewer to deal effectively with several adults at once in this situation, you should decide in advance which parent or parents will participate in the interview.

If you are a divorced parent on good terms with your ex-spouse, for example, and are sharing custody with her, you should both attend the interview.

But if it's possible or likely that the two of you will flare up at each other, you will have to agree on which one of you will go alone to the interview. In that case, it is reasonable to ask the interviewer's permission to tape the discussion for the parent who does not attend.

DO NOT use the interview as an opportunity to discuss your divorce settlement...air your conflicting ideas about child rearing...or complain about custody arrangements.

DO remember that your child, not your ex-spouse, is the subject at hand. You two adults have agreed to meet together because you are the child's principal caregivers and share a genuine interest in his welfare.

Whatever the family situation, aim for a relaxed, friendly, open interview. You are both there to share information and insights about your child...and that can be a pleasure for you both, however you feel about each other.

## WHAT SHOULD BE TAKEN TO THE INTERVIEW?

Only your personal warmth, honesty and goodwill toward your child...

If the admissions officer wants any supplemental information, he'll let you know.  Usually, all of the suitable school records, reports and glowing testimonials have already been submitted along with your application.

One of our clients made the mistake of taking along a packet bulging with examples of her daughter's schoolwork and various accounts of her extracurricular activities.  This is interesting stuff for doting grandparents, but not for an admissions officer. He's seen it before.  It's not likely to be relevant to his decision.

But, if you fervently believe that your child's schoolwork or writing or painting says something important about him, place it in a folder (*not* a briefcase), set the folder aside until an appropriate point in the interview, and then ask the interviewer if she would like to put it with your application to be looked at *later*.  Don't insist that she read or react to the work in your presence.  And please don't read it to her yourself.

## WHAT QUESTIONS CAN YOU EXPECT?

The interviewer and you are allies.  She wants you to be at ease so that you can be the best possible advocate for your child.  She is not trying to trap you.  Think of her questions as opportunities for you to say what you want to say.

"What can you tell us about your child?"

"What do you enjoy most about your child?"

The interview starts with general questions so that you can focus on what you think is important.  Be prepared with the anecdotes that reveal who your child is...illustrate his special strengths...show him dealing with others.

For a five year old, you might want to describe his favorite activities at preschool and what he says about them.

For an older child, you might want to talk about special talents or interests, then explain how you think they might flourish and develop in this new school. Perhaps she's an athletic eighth grader and you've heard that the junior varsity swim team is weak in relays.  Or she sings soprano, and you've heard that the school music teacher is worried about casting the spring musical.

(It certainly can't hurt that this kind of conversation shows that you've done your homework...and suggests that you have specific reasons for applying to this school apart from social cachet or convenience.)

"What skills would you like your child to develop here?"

Don't assume that the school has a preferred answer to this kind of question. For example, many private schools encourage children to develop leadership qualities, but they also understand that many children are not born to lead. These kids are just as important to the school because they can cooperate with their teachers and interact productively with their classmates.

Stick with the truth, whatever you think the educational trends might be. Don't answer that you want your child to develop leadership skills, for example, when that is inappropriate to his personality. Don't claim that you hope he will become a math whiz when his strength lies with English and social studies.

And don't try to flatter the interviewer by acting as if you believe the school can work academic or social miracles with your child. Be reasonable. Be straight.

On the other hand, don't hold back. If you have chosen a school because you are looking for an accelerated academic program for a child who excels only when offered a challenge, don't hesitate to say so. And stress that your motive is to give her the opportunity to experience the satisfaction of doing her best.

"Has she had any special education services? (tutoring, speech therapy, psychological counseling, etc.)"

This question may be difficult for you if your child has ever been in psychological therapy or in remediation for a learning disorder. Just prepare yourself, tell the truth, and explain without apology or embarrassment. The interviewer is an educator, not a judge. He needs to help the school determine what its role can be in meeting your child's special need.

If your daughter is taking speech therapy, for example, briefly describe the course of treatment, explain how much progress she's made and give her therapist's prognosis. Will the therapy continue much longer? Does it take much of her time? Does her problem affect her performance in class or her interactions with other children? Discuss these issues without hesitation.

Whatever the situation, you must make clear that you consider yourself a part of the teaching team that deals with your child's emotional or physical difficulty.

Say it straight out: "We are happy to share any information that we have about Erik's learning style." If you've had a professional evaluation, you can offer those results. You can also talk about any supplemental support Erik has received and give a summary of his progress and accomplishments to date.

As always, be specific. If your four year old bursts into tears when he's asked to try a new activity in pre-school, explain the where, the when, and the how. If he's disciplined in this situation, how does he respond? What does his teacher say about the problem? Does the same thing happen at home? If his behavior pattern is viewed by educators as developmental, he won't be considered a potentially serious problem for the new school. The assumption is that over time the situation will improve and resolve itself.

On the other hand, be realistic. If your child has been diagnosed with a severe, chronic behavior disorder...if he has been sent home from school three days out of five for hitting and biting other children — it is unlikely that most private schools will accept him. This is the time to confer with a qualified expert to determine where your child can find the right educational circumstances. There are schools that will work with you and your child, after he has been professionally evaluated, in order to serve his needs.

"What does your child offer our school?"

Think about this question beforehand and come up with a serious, frank answer. (If the question isn't asked, you can still bring up the subject.)

In a nutshell, this is what the interview is all about. The admissions officer and committee is trying to put together the best possible population mix for the school. Where will your child fit? How will she change the environment...contribute to the community...benefit her classmates and satisfy her teachers...make a mark in academics or sports or theater?

Preparing the answer to this question will help you **decide what you mean to accomplish** during the interview.

"What books influenced you the most in raising your child?"

Most interviewers will ask this question.  It is not meant as a test of your intelligence or parental commitment but as a possible source of insight into your child and your family.  In other words, don't try to fake a response.

Before your interview, glance through your bookshelves or try to recall the names of books that influenced you and your spouse years ago.  Popular examples include *Between Parent & Child*, *Raising a Responsible Child*, *Recipes for Parenting*, and *Practical Steps to Successful Family Relationships*.

## OTHER POSSIBLE QUESTIONS

"What do you know about us and our teaching methods?"

"Why do you think our school is appropriate for your child?"

"What are his greatest strengths?"

"What kinds of things do the two of you do together?"

"What sports does he play?"

"How does the family spend a Saturday?"

"What additional information would you like about us?"

"How does your child react to new situations?

"What are you hoping for your child during elementary school?...middle school?...high school?"

"How does your child play with other children?"

"Is your child fluent in any language other than English?"

As you consider these questions, keep in mind that the school is *not interested in the specific responses*.

For example, it doesn't matter where the family goes for vacation.  The school is interested in how your child answers these and other questions.  The most successful applicants express themselves well...allow their enthusiasm and self-confidence to shine through...demonstrate their reasoning ability (and are not afraid to think aloud)...and behave in ways appropriate to their age — mature, but not inhibited.

## WHAT WILL THEY ASK YOUR CHILD?

With children from middle school age and up, the interviewer will use a question-and-answer format, much as he will with you. In some cases, a question is intended to elicit specific information...in others, to give your child a chance to express her own thoughts or feelings.

**POSITIVE ATTITUDE HINT:** Don't grit your teeth when your child gives an answer you find off-center or incomplete or surprising. Let him and the interviewer interact without interfering. Don't try to edit or explain or dismiss a reply.

(This may be more difficult than you expect. If the interviewer asks why your son is applying, he might reply, "Because Mom made me." Don't worry. To repeat, the interviewer knows the territory.)

Often, the interviewer will interview parent and child separately. Don't worry about it, and don't use the third-degree afterward, even if you're trying to find out something you think might be helpful in an interview at another school. Leave it alone.

Discuss some of the following typical interview questions with your child in a casual, low-key manner. If you think it would make your child more anxious to hear too many of them, just choose one or two. Say something like, "These are some of the questions they might ask you at the school."

She should not try to prepare answers or psych out the interviewer. *Spontaneity and honesty* are the keys to a good interview.

For example, when asked to name a favorite book, it would be better for a kid to talk enthusiastically (and honestly) about a Nancy Drew mystery than to pretend to care about *Silas Marner.*

Do not tell your child to lie in order to impress the interviewer: not about your address, your birthday, your ethnic background, or anything else. Quite apart from morality, such lying always backfires.

(Diplomacy *is* in order for one question: "Is this school your first choice?" If it isn't but you want to keep your options open, your child could answer, "I could really see myself going to school here.")

## SOME POSSIBLE QUESTIONS FOR STUDENTS

"What kind of books do you read?"

"What's your favorite book?"

"What can you tell me about the last book you read?"

"What do you like to do after school?"

"Who are your heroes?"

"What is your favorite subject in school?" "Why?"

"Who is your favorite actor?"

"What is your favorite song?"

"Tell me about your family (friends, pets)."

"Which one person has had the most significant influence on your life so far?"

"What do you like best about your best friend?"

"Why are you interested in this school?"

"What would you change about your current school?" "Why?"

"If you could write your own letter of recommendation, what would you say?"

"What person living or dead would you most like to have lunch with?" "Why?"

"Do you play any sports?"

"Do you have any hobbies?"

"If you do transfer from your old school, what will you miss most about it?"

"Where do you go on vacations?"

"What has been your favorite trip?"

As you can see, the interviewer often prepares a series of related questions, hoping to deal with the predictable problem of monosyllabic or vague replies: "Yeah," "Nope," "I guess," "I don't know."

Talk with your child about this problem before the interview. The secret to a productive interview, though, is not just to give sentence-long answers as much as possible. The secret is to **answer the question behind the question**.

Here's what we mean:

The interviewer asks Amy, "What is your favorite TV show?"

Just giving the title — for example, "Full House" — would be a weak, unproductive answer, because the **question behind the question** is something like this, "Why do you like `Full House' so much?"

Amy should answer the question something like this: "My favorite show is 'Full House', because I like to see how Stephanie handles things. Just like me, she's the middle child in the family."

Or, to take another example, the interviewer asks, "Who do you admire the most?"

Instead of answering "Steffi Graf," Amy should explain **why**: "I love Steffi Graf because she never gives up, even when she seems far behind and the crowd is cheering for someone else."

We are NOT suggesting that your child prepare answers. Instead, she should make a kind of game out of learning to answer the question behind the question.

After all, our experience shows that children usually have fun during these interviews. They aren't feeling the same kinds of pressure the parent might (unless the parents have transferred their own insecurities about the experience). They are the center of a concerned interviewer's attention. They get to think out loud and talk about matters that might otherwise not have occurred to them. They tend to feel proud of themselves for handling the situation.

**POSITIVE ATTITUDE HINTS:** Beforehand, focus on the positives. Explain to your child that the person you are going to meet is really interested in getting to know him...really wants to know about his life.

To repeat, you must not do anything that raises the anxiety levels or frightens your child. This is, after all, just a school interview, not root canal without anesthesia. It only seems that way.

## PROBLEMS IN INTERVIEWING THE YOUNGER CHILD

We find it's best with preschoolers to call the school ahead of time and ask what the interview will be like. For example, will your child be interviewed by herself, or along with other children?... Will she be taken to a separate room?...What kinds of things will she be asked to do?...How long will the interview last?

You might be asked to leave the room at some point or your preschooler might be invited to a separate room. She is likely to be asked to perform some task like catching a ball or coloring a drawing of a geometric triangle. These are not skills tests but opportunities for the interviewer to assess your child's behavior, personality, and ability to follow directions. Does she stand back, or does she participate eagerly in the activity?

If you are allowed to remain in the room, fade into the background. DO NOT offer comments or assistance. DO NOT make hasty armchair interpretations of your child's chances based upon what goes on in front of you.

As preparation for your preschooler, you should do no more in most cases than explain what is likely to happen...and assure her that it is going to be fun.

But there are *two fairly common problem areas* that you can anticipate and work on:

1.   SEPARATION ANXIETY

    If your child is prone to separation anxiety when you leave him, visualize with him the moment when you are going to walk out of the interview room (or he is taken to a separate room). Go over the details, as you have learned them from the school.  Tell them there will be two games, say, if you know the interviewer plans two separate exercises.  Remind him that you will be in the next room all the time.

*Avoid "prep overkill"*.  One father focused his energies on preparing his son to go off confidently with the interviewer, forgetting to discuss the tasks that were coming.  The boy was so focused on being able to leave his father that he had no concentration or interest left for the interview.

2.  WILLING PARTICIPATION

To help your child understand what is going to happen and feel relaxed about it, you can drive by the school before the interview.  "We're going to go there soon," you might say, "and a teacher will ask you questions and play some games with you."

*Don't set up false expectations*. Hoping to get her five year old son excited about the interview, one mother pointed out the state-of-the-art playground equipment outside the school.  When they went for their appointment, the boy raced joyously to the playground and had to be dragged away in tears. He wasn't to blame. What to her was a selling point was to him a promise of playtime.

She should have said, "This is the school we'll be visiting tomorrow.  It has a lot of fun things like that great slide and swings, and lots of books and nice rooms for schoolwork.  We probably won't get a chance to play tomorrow, but we are going to meet with one of the teachers and have fun inside."

In today's society, we generally warn our children to be wary of talking to strangers, and some children go through a stage of being suspicious of personal questions. Make sure your child knows that the interviewer will ask questions for a good reason and it will be OK to cooperate.

## LOOKING RIGHT

The initial impression your child makes is important, perhaps irreversible. The proper appearance is a crucial part of that impression.

1. This is not a debutante ball. Avoid the lace party dress or spanking new Brooks Brothers boys suit. Over-dressing indicates a misunderstanding of the purpose of the interview.

2. BUT make sure your child is clean and neatly groomed. Her appearance reflects upon you both.

3. The best outfit is one your child finds comfortable and fun to wear — within reason. You, your child and the interviewer will all know what your community thinks about various styles of dress. It won't hurt to follow the rules. Clothes send a loud message.

4. Body language is just as expressive. Children of any age should use good posture and try to make eye contact. Teenagers really can refrain from slumping in a chair and staring passively at the floor — at least for a brief interview. Younger children can be taught not to suck their thumbs, crawl under the table or pick their noses.

But do not make the mistake of over preparing your child. Do not try to "script" the interview.

## WHAT QUESTIONS SHOULD YOU ASK?

No matter how much you know about the school, *you can always learn more*.

*Ask for examples and samples.* If you ask a general question like "What kind of homework will my son have?", the reply is not likely to be very helpful. Instead, ask to see a copy of a typical science homework assignment.

*What about discipline?* Schools, like parents, have different philosophies in this area. To avoid subsequent misunderstandings, we strongly urge you to ask the interviewer how teachers in her school handle discipline. What methods or punishments are considered appropriate? Are the parents involved?

Similarly, you want to find out *how conflicts between students are resolved*. What do you have to ask about this problem? Think back to your own experiences in school...and you will know.

*What about fundraising?* It is reasonable to ask about your and your child's responsibilities for helping the school raise money, because these activities can be demanding on your schedule as well as your bank account.  Students might be expected to sell items, and you might be expected to solicit pledges.  Find out for certain.  (It is wise to ask this question of parents already involved in the school.  For example, the pressure to contribute a "suggested" amount to the building fund can result in significant "hidden costs".)

***What about religious affiliations?***  In some circumstances, you might want to know more about a school's actual responsibilities to its religious sponsorship.  For example, is anyone restricted from enrollment because of this affiliation?  Are church members given priority?

## WHEN THE INTERVIEW BOMBS!

It happens.

After the interview, ask your child how she feels about the experience: kids often know exactly when they've passed with flying colors...and when they've bombed.

If she is concerned, react calmly.  DO NOT dismiss her interpretation out of hand...and DO NOT agree wholeheartedly.  Your role is to avoid making her feel worse about the situation, which *might* be better than she thinks.  Do not try to second-guess the interviewer yourself.  The interviewer may feel that it is very important not to give away their true feelings in the interview situation.

Without expressing false hopes, you could say something like, "Sometimes you can't tell what they really feel"....or, "You did your best, and that was probably just what they wanted."  Remember, there is no such thing as a "right" or a "wrong" answer in the interview.

Don't make a bad situation worse with foolish responses like, "They are stuck-up and snobbish here, and I wouldn't go here if they paid me"...or, "They call *this* a school?  How dare they?"...or, "Where do they get these idiots who do these interviews? Anyway, she wasn't anyone to worry about.  We didn't get the head of admissions."  (Sad to say, these are actual responses we've learned about.)

Most importantly, focus on helping her see the interview as one more experience of many to come in life.  It's done.  It's over.  She should move on to the next thing.

BUT if she continues to worry, she could take some action that will help her feel she's left no stone unturned. She might write a brief, straightforward letter to the admissions director that provides information that was not covered during the interview. This should give her a sense of closure.

**CASE STUDY:** Make certain she understands that she may not receive a personal reply. Alan, a young boy we saw in our office, wanted desperately to go to art school but felt that he was unconvincing in his interview.

With his mother's encouragement, he wrote a very thoughtful, specific letter to the admissions office, telling things about himself and his love of art that had not come up during the interview. He was devastated when there was no response.

YOU may be the one with the problem when an interview does not go well. Even the most sensitive child will eventually move beyond the experience, which will be a tiny part of his entire school life.

But you may be one of those parents — and they are legion — who continue to obsess about a a failed interview.

The worst offenders go on and on in great detail with friends and relatives, even within hearing range of the child...or question their child's friends about their own experiences with interviews. This is self-centered, pointless behavior that hurts your child's self-esteem. Avoid it at all costs!

## SUMMING UP: SOME INTERVIEW DO'S AND DON'TS

DO offer your support as a volunteer for school activities.
Explain specifically how you think you can contribute as a team player: for example, helping coach a sport you know or like well, helping with a extracurricular club's car pool, tutoring, arranging for guest speakers, or whatever.

DO NOT bring up financial issues during the interview.
The school will have a financial officer or other staff member designated to handle such discussions.

Most schools will have sent out information about tuition fees, payment schedules and possible financial assistance along with the application packet.

DO take note that admissions personnel are likely to be extremely sensitive to appearances of conflict.

After a promising interview, one family almost automatically sent the admissions officer a bouquet of flowers as a gesture of appreciation. What would ordinarily be considered courtesy was in this case misconstrued as an attempt to gain influence. Their daughter was rejected.

(On the other hand, do not be afraid to thank an interviewer for his time and concern, or for making you and your child feel comfortable.)

DO NOT let your eagerness to get your child accepted undermine the interview. If you can afford to build the school a new gym, keep it to yourself. (The word is "bribe".) One of our clients, a self-made hard-driving executive, felt totally helpless when he found himself at the mercy of a school admissions officer. His money had always paved the way for him, but his offer of $1 million to the building fund got him nowhere. You may be a Fortune 500 executive used to being in control, but you don't have a seat on the admissions committee.

DO remain positive after an interview that does not seem to go well. Learn from the experience; try to understand what went wrong; plan to avoid such mistakes when you go to the next interview. If the interview seemed to be a success, think about what went well and why so that you can repeat the triumph.

## CHAPTER 8

# THE AGONY AND THE ECSTASY: ACCEPTANCE/REJECTION

Now it is decision time: you've completed all of your assignments, and you await the decisions of the public and/or private schools of your choice. Try to relax as the anticipation builds during this exciting time. Talking to one person may make you feel better about your chances; talking to another may make you feel worse. Your emotions will see-saw between the hope of getting your first choice and the fear of being rejected.

Chances are, you personally did not experience the kind of pressure you might now feel for your child until you applied to college. If you are feeling at sea, don't worry. Like many other people, you are having to deal with the fallout of tremendous changes in the way American children are educated.

**POSITIVE ATTITUDE HINT:** *Keep it all in perspective*. With competition so fierce, acceptance/rejection is to some extent a numbers game, a gamble. Recognize that there is an element of chance in the admissions process, and many unpredictable, uncontrollable human factors are involved.

Life isn't fair, and the admissions process in certain instances won't be fair, no matter how well intentioned the admissions officers may be. People with better connections, or with children already in the school, or with more money in the bank may get the special edge. Sometimes, it's simply a matter of different styles of being.

Above all, remember that rejection — or acceptance, for that matter — is *not a judgment of you or your child as a human being*.

## HOW YOU GET THE NEWS

Typically, all letters of acceptance/rejection are mailed by the schools on the same day.  You and your child will probably have a good idea when the news is likely to arrive.

We suggest that you plan to *get to the mailbox first*, so that you can process your feelings about the verdict before conveying the news to your child.  Whether he has been accepted or rejected, a milestone has been passed in his life...and in yours.

Some parents, we've found, need a few hours or a few days to let the whole thing sink in.  They may want to calm down from their own delight with acceptance before telling their child about it, because they don't want to overwhelm her reaction.  Or, if the reply is a rejection, they may want to work through their own grief so that they can be more supportive of their child.

## YOU GOT IN

Celebrate the moment! Enjoy the triumph!

This should be one of the happiest days in your child's life, when the future seems filled with nothing but possibility and promise.  You deserve to share the joy as well, of course, and so do all of the people who helped out by writing recommendations or were supportive in any other way.

Nothing should dampen your pleasure, but you should help your child understand a couple of issues that make acceptance a complex experience:

1. One or more of your child's **best friends may not have been accepted**. Face this fact positively by saying something like, "We're so excited and happy, but Stephanie and Emily may feel disappointed for a while.  What can we do to make them feel better?"

   Your child will learn a valuable lesson: the winners are happiest when everyone else wins, too, and sincerely want to comfort those who have been rejected.

2. Don't congratulate your child so giddily that he feels he can never fail again.  If you say (with the best intentions in the world), "You're so spe-

cial they couldn't resist you," how is he going to feel when he's    not near the top of the class or a standout in sports at the new school?

Make sure that your pride in him today does not put pressure on him to feel that he has to be perfect ever afterward.

## IF YOU ARE FORTUNATE ENOUGH TO RECEIVE MANY ACCEPTANCES

You and your child are very fortunate to have *multiple acceptances*. No one's going to sympathize if you think that such good fortune presents a problem...but it can. [This is just between you and us; it would be very insensitive to complain aloud, especially when so many other children may be experiencing rejection.]

How do you choose?

1.  *Consider the next likely step* after this one...Yes, in some cases, a certain kindergarten is on a faster track toward a certain kind of middle school and high school — and even college — than another equally competent kindergarten. The school you choose can be like a "branching" decision on a CD-ROM...or like Robert Frost's decision in "The Road Not Taken." If you are new to a community, talk with other parents about the probable academic impact of your choice.

2.  *Consider what the total curriculum* offers your child in particular. Don't be swayed by a school's reputation for academics, if the program is slanted away from your child's special interests. Choose the program that is most likely to excite your child from now until graduation.

3.  Consider which school will *be the most supportive of your child and your family*. Some schools can become intrusive in child raising...others say, "You love 'em, we teach 'em"...and still others want to work together with you in helping your child learn and grow. Each of these approaches will work with some children. Try for the best match between the school's attitudes and your family's needs.

    *Strike a balance*: if your child is likely to thrive in a very loosely structured school but you are uncomfortable without firmer guidelines (or vice versa), choose the compromise school that will make you both happy. Otherwise, your discomfort will be communicated to your child.

4.  ***Consider the geographic factor***. If getting your child to a certain school is going to involve a demanding schedule of rush-hour driving or early morning sprints to a bus stop or train station, you may want to strike that choice.  Commuting can tire out your child, who needs the energy for homework and other activities.  It can exhaust and burden you both physically and emotionally.

The factor you should NOT consider crucial is whether or not your child's best friends go to a particular school.

## YOU GOT IN — BUT YOU HAVE SECOND THOUGHTS

What if, after all the hard work and suspense and decision making of the application process, your child is accepted...and THEN you realize that the match is wrong?

***Don't hesitate to make a graceful exit.***

Take responsibility for making a mistake...leave the door open...but ***don't*** enroll your child in a school just because everyone else wants to go there.

***Write a very gentle letter*** thanking the school for their time and concern.  You don't want to burn any bridges.

"We feel very honored and grateful," you might write, "that you have offered Jonathan a place at your school, but we have come to realize that he may not be ready for this step at this time.  We hope that your committee will view our application favorably in the future."

## YOU GOT IN — BUT YOUR CHILD REFUSES TO GO

It's not easy when you are ecstatic that your child has been accepted into the school that you think is perfect for her...and she refuses to go.

**CASE STUDIES:**  Unhappy with the socialization policies and Rachel's lack of friends at one school, her mother applied for her to transfer.  Rachel was accepted but refused to make the change. "I won't have Hebrew school at the new place," she protested.  "And I'll miss my friends."  What should her mother do?

Nine year old Michael's parents thought he was getting academically lost in public school. His teacher complained that he could not easily follow directions and was slow to complete work. They visited a private school and were encouraged by the small size of the classes and the school's willingness to pay special attention to their son's difficulties. An opening happened to be available, but the boy refused to transfer, mostly because he didn't want to leave his friends. The parents became anxious, because the admissions director could not guarantee them a spot the next year. Michael began to feel such stress that he began habitually picking at his face. How can this dilemma be solved?

There are no quick, predictable, easy answers to this kind of problem. Sometimes, the parents feel under tremendous pressure to grab a coveted spot, often under deadline pressure, but subjecting a child to severe stress and anxiety is too high a price to pay.

It is not unusual for children to resist change — quite the contrary. Stability is very comforting. But when you feel strongly that a school transfer is in your child's best interest, work patiently with her to help her develop a positive attitude toward the situation.

Avoid a crisis, with your child screaming, "You can't make me go!" Keep it calm, and assure her that you will work together as a family to come up with the answer that is best all around.

1. As an aid to discussion — not as the deciding factor, by any means — *list the pros and cons* of making the change.

   You might find that 20 items on the "con" side outweigh one on the "pro" side, or vice versa. Katy might object that transfer means a long commute, loss of friends, a less advanced French class, and so forth. But you offer the more varied curriculum as a selling point. As you discuss the proper balance of these factors, Katy may agree with your point of view. Be inventive: for example, talk about long-range goals versus short-range goals.

2. Your child cannot immediately grasp, without your explanation, what transfer *means for the future*. You can agree that her present school has many wonderful things to offer, but talk about how the new school is more likely to lead her toward the kind of experiences she will want to have in high school, college and beyond.

*Perfection is unlikely*: It may be that your child, like many other children, will never fully enjoy the experience of school...but he can learn to tolerate it. If the problem is with "school" rather than with a particular school, a transfer may not help. In that case, hop-scotching from one school to the next may be more damaging than dealing openly and sensibly with his discontent about school in general.

## ADAPTING TO THE NEW SCHOOL

Even when children and parents are very excited about a transfer to a new school, problems can arise. *When expectations are unreasonably high*, even a very good experience may be perceived as a disappointment...

**CASE STUDIES:** Jessica couldn't wait for opening day at her new school. She was sure she'd have five new friends by the end of the week. When this rosy fantasy proved false, she came home weeping bitterly. Luckily, her mother realized that overly high expectations are normal...and it's just as normal for them to hit the skids during the adaptation process. She encouraged Jessica to talk about her disappointment and to come up with a more realistic goal for becoming part of the new school.

Unfortunately, we've encountered parents who were not so wise. Some make the mistake of intervening at school to try to make their child's fantasies come true right away. Others become frustrated and blame their child, saying such things as, "I jumped through all these hoops to get you into that school, and now you're blowing it!" In this case, it may be the parent who had the rosy fantasy.

*During the adaptation process*, listen to your child's complaints. Don't be afraid that you are encouraging him to give up if you talk out his unhappiness.

On the contrary, you can *help him put things in perspective*. For example, you can discuss whether it's better to have five casual friends right away, or one really important friendship that takes time to develop.

Make sure that you are not dismissing his feelings because you are so pleased yourself about his acceptance to the school. As one child put it, "Daddy is so excited about this school I wish I could send him here instead."

## WHAT ABOUT THE OLD SCHOOL?

The *short-timer phenomenon* — although it's rare — can occur when a child thinks that acceptance to a new school means that she can write off her current school...even when there are three or four months of classwork to go.

The capable student goes soft on homework...the well-behaved child gets into fights...the respectful student begins to ignore the teacher, saying something like, "Why should I listen to you, when I'm never going to see you again?"

Perhaps this phenomenon reveals that a child has been under much more stress during the application process than anyone realized. Talk with her to see if that's the case.

But whatever the reason, this kind of behavior can be self-destructive. Remind your child that acceptance to the new school is contingent on her successfully completing her work in the current school: generally speaking, the school contract spells out this proviso. Underline it, if necessary, and pin it to the refrigerator door.

Teachers will be on the lookout for this reaction. Your child has not earned a vacation from learning. Growth is a non-stop process.

## BUT WHAT IF...YOU DIDN'T MAKE IT

To repeat, rejection of your child's application is *not rejection of her as a human being*. *Make sure you believe that*...then get the message across to her.

It is also *not a rejection of you*. One mother told us that her son received nothing but rejection letters on the fatal day. Laughing, she said, "I've never received so many nice letters rejecting me in one day in my whole life." She was joking, but there is truth in humor: in this case, she was making the serious mistake of identifying herself too closely with her son and his life. You're not the issue here.

**CASE STUDY:** Another mother was upset because her son was rejected by the school that she and her clique considered to be "politically correct." She was embarrassed for herself and for her entire family because "all of our friends got accepted, and we did not."

In this case, she asked friends to use their influence to have her son spend a few hours at the school with his prospective classmates. His application was denied a second time. She pushed him to apply a third time, with the same results.

Her persistence, of course, could be seen as a good thing in some circumstances. Here, it became an embarrassment for her son and his friends.

## PREPARE YOUR CHILD

This woman did not follow our advice *to build a safety net for your child and yourself*, just in case.

1. Have alternatives in mind so that you can regroup quickly. You know what happens when you put all of your eggs in one basket...Drop it, and you have a gooey mess.

2. Plan how to help your child deal with the denial of his application.

This is not negative thinking; it is *sensible preparation for damage control*.

## SELL THE ALTERNATIVE

Get excited about the place where your child WILL be going to school!

Some children *misunderstand* the rejection letter; they think it means they will not be going to school at all. From now on, change your focus to the school where your child will actually be going.

1. *Talk about all the good things* available at that school...the friends who will be going there...the teacher who was so friendly...your own eagerness to visit during special assemblies or sports events.

    *Remember:* it is hard for children to go somewhere six hours a day if they have a feeling in the pit of their stomachs that they should be disappointed or ashamed to be going there.

2. *Take action and visit the school*. If possible, meet soon with your child's teacher for the coming year. If the three of you can meet together, the teacher will probably handle the situation by coming up with "teasers". "See those battery-operated robots?" he might say. "We always build

them from scratch as a midwinter science project.  Each student gets to choose the kind of materials he wants to use."

## OR...YOU'RE ON THE WAITING LIST

In any situation at any age, a **waiting list** can seem to be a special kind of purgatory.  Face that fact squarely with an older child: the suspense will continue...and you will have to continue to invest your energies in the alternatives.

But do not hesitate to *find out exactly what is going on*.  Are you third in line while the school gives its first-choice applicants a week or month to make up their minds?  Depending upon the community and the popularity of the school, that might not be a weak position, after all.  You shouldn't encourage false expectations, though.  Dealing with this kind of uncertainty, if you handle it calmly, can help your child develop toward maturity.

You can take certain concrete steps:

1.  You and an older child should decide together how you want to deal with the waiting list.  Is the school your No. 1 or No. 5 choice?  How much emotion do you want to invest in hanging on? Don't assume that she feels the same way you do.

2.  If the school is important to you both, you could write a letter explaining how you feel and expressing your hope that there will be an opening in the future.

Your child should explain that she understands that no spot is available at the moment, then emphasize that she still wants very much to attend the school. Briefly, she could note some specific reasons she believes that the school will be good for her, and vice versa.  Perhaps she can recall a conversation she had there with a student or a class she attended: for example, "I'll never forget hearing Mr. Truffino tell his class about the ancient Egyptians.  He made it sound so exciting, and I wanted to learn more."

In your letter, affirm that the school is your first choice and you want to be actively considered on the waiting list.  If you have friends whose children already attend the school, ask them to drop a casual note on your behalf or to speak to a teacher who regards them well.  Your goal is to remind the school that you are sincerely interested...to come across as excited about your child's chances of being accepted...to show that you want to be involved in the school community.

**CASE STUDY:** In his letter, one young man wrote that he would be happy to come in again to meet with the admissions officer. As he put it, the school probably had so many applicants that they had forgotten what he looked like. His amusing, straightforward letter enchanted the school. He was soon accepted.

## SPECIAL CIRCUMSTANCES: THE DEADLINE CRUNCH

What if your child is *accepted by your second- or third-choice school* — which demands a reply and a non refundable deposit within the week — but your first-choice school is not going to send out acceptance/rejection letters before that deadline date?

Quite frankly, you're in a terrible dilemma. You can try to stall, of course, but that will soon result in feelings of bad faith between you and the school.

In the best of all possible worlds, you should be able to discuss the situation honestly with the school. Explain that you feel that School X might be a better match for your child and you would like to wait for their reply because you are trying to make the decision that is best for him. In our view, the best schools will understand you when you speak from the heart in this very difficult situation.

Unfortunately, the second-choice school might be trying to build a reputation by forcing top-quality students to make early-admission decisions. Or they may feel that they don't want students who consider them second-choice.

We hope you don't have to face this dilemma. If you do, keep the problem on the home front. If you begin discussing your options with other people, you are bound to be dizzied with the overload of their varying opinions.

## SHOULD YOU REAPPLY, WHEN REJECTED?

Most schools look very favorably upon reapplication. It shows that you are sincerely interested in what they have to offer, not just shopping around. It suggests that you understand that it is very difficult for them to grant acceptance to everyone who is qualified:

1.  Reapply as soon as the next year's forms are available so the school won't think you are making a last-minute decision.

2.  Politely reply to this year's letter of rejection by return mail, if possible.

    Write something like, "We understand that there is no room for Jennifer this year, but she is eager to be reconsidered next year. Please notify us when we can reapply."

## FALSE PROMISES?

You might be told that your child has been rejected this year but *should reapply the following year*. What if, a year later, he is rejected again?

Strictly speaking, the school made no promises. On the other hand, you are certain that acceptance was implied, at least vaguely.

There is, frankly, no completely comfortable resolution to this problem. Did he disappoint the school's expectations during the intervening year? Was there a sudden upsurge in the quality of competing applicants? Did the school's goals and policies change during the year? Was there miscommunication because an admissions officer tried to let you down politely?

If you can deal with the school in a non confrontational manner, it could be very helpful both to you and your child to get some answers. You need to sort out exactly what happened. The school staff also needs to learn how this situation occurred: it's not in their interest to seem to make promises that are not fulfilled.

However you choose to deal with the situation, keep your older child informed. You want her to understand that you are not blaming her for this disappointment.

## DECISIONS

As you see from this chapter, the direct responses of "accepted" or "rejected" are only the tip of the iceberg. Quite a few other possibilities, many of them ambiguous and demanding on your patience, are possible.

If you find the process of finding the right school for your child more painful than you expected, if you begin to feel helpless and inadequate beyond proportion to the circumstances, you might want to consider consulting a professional.

This could be a time of excitement and possibility, along with a dose of reasonable expectations. If it begins to turn sour, neither you nor your child will benefit.

It's much more likely, we believe, that you will both have a positive experience and will someday look back fondly upon your many challenges and discoveries throughout the school-choice process.

We hope that our book has been helpful during your search and wish you the very best.

And now to the next plateau... Keep an eye out for our next book, *Secrets to School Success: Guiding Your Child to a Joyous Learning Experience.*

# ABOUT THE AUTHORS

## BRANDI ROTH, PH.D.

Dr. Brandi Roth is an action oriented psychologist in private practice in Beverly Hills, California. She specializes in conflict resolution with families, individuals, adolescents and children. She also assists young children and adolescents with academic and behavioral problems

Her experience as counselor, educator, advocate, classroom teacher, program administrator and staff developer give Dr. Roth additional insight into many aspects of human behavior.

Dr. Roth is an advisor to several therapeutic and educational organizations. She is also a popular seminar and media lecturer.

### EDUCATION
Ph.D., Counseling Psychology, Professional School of Psychological Studies
M.A., Counseling Psychology, Professional School of Psychological Studies
B.A., Sociology, California State University, Long Beach

### PROFESSIONAL LICENSES & CERTIFICATES
Psychologist, California License
Standard Life Teaching Credential, California
Specialist in the Learning Handicapped, Life Credential, California
Certificate in Vision, Vision Screening and Reading

## PROFESSIONAL EXPERIENCE

Psychological Private Practice since 1990

Educator since 1968

Consultant and Lecturer, public & private sector

## DR. ROTH'S STATEMENT

I am a psychologist with extensive background and experience in most areas of education, including teaching for 15 years, program specialist with Los Angeles City Schools, a degree in special education, and I have a long history as an advocate for gifted and special-needs children.

My practice includes working on psychological issues with children and adults, counseling, lecturing, and neuropsychological evaluations. One of the most exciting parts of my practice is being able to match children and schools. As a psychologist, I have integrated all of my education and experience to contribute to this matching process. I act as a guide to the best school placement for children.

I support parents through the emotional turbulence which sometimes surrounds the decision-making process when they are choosing a school for their children. I assist with the associated emotional issues that may arise. I evaluate children's academic and emotional needs. I guide parent conferences, speak with teachers, help select programs for the special needs of a child, and function as a resource for the educators.

# FAY VAN DER KAR-LEVINSON, PH.D.

Dr. Fay Van Der Kar-Levinson, a psychologist in private practice in West Los Angeles, California, specializes in matching individual learning styles with appropriate educational programs.  As a child development expert, Dr. Van Der Kar-Levinson provides consultation and support for the parents of young children.  As a parent, she has had direct experience with the joys and pitfalls of being actively involved in her child's education.

## EDUCATION
Ph.D., Educational Psychology, University of California at Los Angeles
M.A., Learning & Development, University of California at Los Angeles
B.A., Psychology, University of Southern California

## PROFESSIONAL LICENSES & CERTIFICATES
Clinical Psychologist
Member American Psychological Association

## PROFESSIONAL EXPERIENCE
Private Practice since 1979
Visiting Assistant Professor, Special Education, Pepperdine University,
Los Angeles, 1977–1979
Adjunct Professor, UCLA Extension, since 1976
Consultant & Lecturer, schools, parent organizations, professional
organizations

## DR. VAN DER KAR-LEVINSON'S STATEMENT

I am a Clinical Psychologist with extensive experience working with children, parents, and schools.

Often, I play the roles of detective and matchmaker; taking an in-depth look at the child to identify a profile and a learning style and match this style to a school or program.

Assisting families through the process of finding the right school for their child has been a natural outcome of my long time interest in how children learn and develop.

Working together with pediatricians, teachers, school administrators, neurologists, and speech pathologists to design treatment programs for children remains an exciting and important part of my practice.

## FEEDBACK AND QUESTIONS

We are planning to provide follow-up information. Please take a few moments to write to us and give us your comments and feedback.

• How did you use this book in selecting a school for your child?

_____
_____
_____
_____
_____
_____
_____
_____
_____
_____

• Which part was most helpful to you?

_____
_____
_____
_____
_____
_____
_____
_____
_____
_____

• What additional part(s) would you like included in our next book?

_____
_____
_____
_____
_____
_____
_____
_____
_____
_____

• What words of advice or suggestions would you make to other parents?

_____
_____
_____
_____
_____
_____
_____
_____
_____

• What questions would you like to ask us?

_____
_____
_____
_____
_____
_____
_____
_____
_____
_____

• Mail your comments to:
    Brandi Roth Ph.D.
    Association of Ideas Publishing
    433 North Camden Drive, Suite 1128
    Beverly Hills, CA 90210

**COMING SOON . . .**

**SECRETS TO SCHOOL SUCCESS:**
**GUIDING YOUR CHILD TO A JOYOUS LEARNING EXPERIENCE**

After your child is admitted to school, decisions, such as the selection of classes and extracurricular activities, and the day-to-day projects, such as homework, provide another opportunity for parents to help their children reach their full potential.

Now that your child is enrolled in the school of your choice, we offer suggestions to help ensure that the educational experience will be a success. This second book guides you to a satisfactory learning experience in the new school. Above all, you want your child's educational experience to be a positive one.

Information about your power and responsibilities as a parent, differing learning styles, scheduling your child's after-school life, and carpooling will be invaluable for you.

We believe that parents must be involved in their children's education, and to do so effectively, they must also be informed. This means understanding who your children are and understanding their educational needs. Our book is designed to help you achieve that understanding.

After a school is selected and admission has been offered, special efforts to help the child with the transition into the new school brings immediate and life-long rewards. The tools for making the child's transition into the new school successful are explained.

*Secrets to School Success* guides parents and child through the student's first year at the new school. For many children, this period of transition sets the tone, both academically and emotionally, of their academic future. Parents learn how to handle the many questions and problems this transition can bring. Most important, they come to understand what "parent power" can and should be. This increased understanding of their children's emotional and academic needs will not only help the children succeed in school but also strengthen the family bonds.

# ORDER FORM

To order your copies of *CHOOSING THE RIGHT SCHOOL FOR YOUR CHILD* by Brandi Roth, Ph.D. & Fay Van Der Kar-Levinson, Ph.D.

## MAIL ORDER FORM AND PAYMENT TO

Association of Ideas Publishing
Brandi Roth, Ph.D.
433 N. Camden Dr., Suite 1128
Beverly HIlls, CA 90210

## PLEASE SHIP TO

Name _____

Title or Business _____

Address _____

City _____ State _____ Zip _____ – _____

Telephone Number ( ) _____

## PRICE

$15.00

## SHIPPING & HANDLING

Book Rate: $2.00 for the first book and 75¢ for each additional book.

## SALES TAX

Please add 8.25% ($1.24) for each book shipped to a California address.

_____ Book(s) Ordered at $15.00:  $_____

Shipping & Handling:  $_____

Sales Tax (California only):  $_____

TOTAL ENCLOSED:  $_____

## PAYMENT ENCLOSED

Please make check or money order payable to:  Association of Ideas Publishing.

❏ Please keep me informed of other books as they become available.

(Please feel free to make copies of this order form for other concerned parents.)

# ORDER FORM

To order your copies of *CHOOSING THE RIGHT SCHOOL FOR YOUR CHILD* by Brandi Roth, Ph.D. & Fay Van Der Kar-Levinson, Ph.D.

## MAIL ORDER FORM AND PAYMENT TO

Association of Ideas Publishing
Brandi Roth, Ph.D.
433 N. Camden Dr., Suite 1128
Beverly HIlls, CA 90210

## PLEASE SHIP TO

Name _____

Title or Business _____

Address _____

City _____ State _____ Zip _____ – _____

Telephone Number ( ) _____

## PRICE

$15.00

## SHIPPING & HANDLING

Book Rate: $2.00 for the first book and 75¢ for each additional book.

## SALES TAX

Please add 8.25% ($1.24) for each book shipped to a California address.

_____ Book(s) Ordered at $15.00: $ _____

Shipping & Handling: $ _____

Sales Tax (California only): $ _____

TOTAL ENCLOSED: $ _____

## PAYMENT ENCLOSED

Please make check or money order payable to: Association of Ideas Publishing.

❑ Please keep me informed of other books as they become available.

(Please feel free to make copies of this order form for other concerned parents.)

# ORDER FORM

To order your copies of *CHOOSING THE RIGHT SCHOOL FOR YOUR CHILD* by Brandi Roth, Ph.D. & Fay Van Der Kar-Levinson, Ph.D.

## MAIL ORDER FORM AND PAYMENT TO

Association of Ideas Publishing
Brandi Roth, Ph.D.
433 N. Camden Dr., Suite 1128
Beverly HIlls, CA 90210

## PLEASE SHIP TO

Name _____

Title or Business _____

Address _____

City _____ State _____ Zip _____ – _____

Telephone Number ( ) _____

## PRICE

$15.00

## SHIPPING & HANDLING

Book Rate: $2.00 for the first book and 75¢ for each additional book.

## SALES TAX

Please add 8.25% ($1.24) for each book shipped to a California address.

_____ Book(s) Ordered at $15.00: $ _____

Shipping & Handling: $ _____

Sales Tax (California only): $ _____

TOTAL ENCLOSED: $ _____

## PAYMENT ENCLOSED

Please make check or money order payable to: Association of Ideas Publishing.

❑ Please keep me informed of other books as they become available.

(Please feel free to make copies of this order form for other concerned parents.)